CW01501581

Pantheon: The Irish is a thoroughly researched introduction to a multi-faceted and often misunderstood mythos and culture. Morgan Daimler provides much-needed clarification regarding the Irish pantheon as distinct from the broad, generic "Celtic" label that's so popular in the Pagan community. In that process, the Irish mythos shines with its own unique, complex beauty. Highly recommended both for readers seeking information for spiritual practice and those interested in the religious history and culture.

Laura Perry, founder and Temple Mom of Ariadne's Tribe (inclusive Minoan spirituality) and author of *Pantheon: The Minoans*

Precise, nuanced, surprisingly fresh, *Pantheon: The Irish* is a resource I will return to again and again. From broad strokes of cultural history, mythology (including a section on moralities discernible in the tales), ritual and magic, to nuggets of lore and a way of organising the material that sweeps away much confusion, Daimler once again gives us an insightful, honest, and thought-provoking path into the complex and beautiful territory that is Irish paganism.

Mael Brigde, author of *A Brigit of Ireland Devotional: Sun Among Stars*

Morgan Daimler is a consistent voice of reason and wisdom and a true gift to modern Paganism. *Pantheon: The Irish* is another crucial piece of that gift. If you are interested in mythology and lore, get it. If you are interested in Irish history and mythology, get it. If you are reading this endorsement, get the book. Get this necessary book.

Courtney Weber, author of *The Morrigan: Celtic Goddess of Magick and Might* and *Hekate: Goddess of Witches*

Morgan Daimler's *Pantheon: The Irish* is an essential read for anyone interested in the rich tapestry of Irish paganism. With deep respect for cultural nuance and a keen eye for detail, Daimler navigates the complex history, beliefs, and practices of the Irish pantheon. This book is not just an introduction; it's a call to genuinely engage with and honor the distinct traditions of Irish paganism. Daimler's work is a beacon for both newcomers and seasoned practitioners, offering a fresh perspective on an ancient belief system. A must-read for anyone eager to explore the authentic roots of Irish spirituality.

Christy Nicholas, author of *The Druid's Brooch* series

Another brilliant book from Morgan Daimler, a leading expert on the traditional lore of Ireland. *Pantheon: The Irish* covers the history, mythology, cosmology, festivals, and deities of the land's rich pagan past. It's packed with superb research in a succinct and easy-to-read style. This is essential reference material for anyone wanting to learn about Ancient Irish beliefs and how people can appropriately use them today.

Lucya Starza, author of the Pagan Portals titles *Candle Magic, Poppets and Magical Dolls, Guided Visualisations*, and *Scrying*, and the Gothic novel *Erosion*

Morgan Daimler's *Pantheon: The Irish* is an introduction to a pantheon that isn't one of the easiest ones to explore. She manages to untangle the different layers to it, with clarity and honesty, being generous with references and directing the seeker to the path to follow from these pages on. Because Irish paganism is hard to follow without getting lost in the dark 'Celtic' forest, plus she also tackles the evolution of some deities into Christian cults. For a good first serious approach to Pre-Christian Irish religion and a must for anyone looking to tune their base and understanding of the Irish pantheon.

Ness Bosch, author of *Sacred Bones, Magic Bones*

Pantheon: The Irish is a thorough introduction to Irish paganism as a living tradition rooted into a mythological past, yet with fruit-bearing branches leaning into our present. Visionary practices, use of herbs, incorporating magic into everyday living, celebrating life events – to name just a few among the topics covered – take the reader on a marvelous journey and facilitate the connection with Irish traditions through deeper understanding, cultural appreciation and respect.

Daniela Simina, author of *Where Fairies Meet: Parallels between Irish and Romanian Fairy Traditions*

I highly recommend this book for anyone who has an interest in following the Irish Pagan Tradition or is interested in the subject from an academic point of view. The author clearly defines what makes the Irish Celtic Tradition unique from the Celtic traditions of the mainland. She gives a clear explanation of the deities and beings woven through a rich mythology that inspired the festivals and rites of the people. Morgan demonstrates from her own personal practice how to incorporate these practices in present-day paganism while glimpsing into the Ogham, giving

her own interpretation of this ancient system. This book has all you need to get started on the path as well as further resources for the journey. An enjoyable read and one for the bookshelf.
Martha Gray, author of *Grimalkyn: The Witches Cat* and *Nine's a Charm*

Morgan Daimler's *Pantheon: The Irish*, is, as you would expect from a writer of her calibre, an enlightening and well-crafted book. Written with proficiency and a lifetime of dedication, Morgan is the ideal teacher to guide anyone seeking to build a relationship with the Irish gods. I was particularly impressed with Morgan's concise clarification of some of the complicated cosmology, such as the lack of clear evidential sources for both creation and destruction. My curiosity was further piqued by the Irish Triads featured at the start of each chapter – these thought-provoking nuggets of knowledge inspired me to investigate further, and I am betting any reader will be as engrossed as I was. Complimented by exemplary research into the mythology and folkloric history of Ireland, Morgan's own personal experience of working with the Irish deities, makes this work a powerful and exciting addition to your library.
Thea Prothero, author of *A Guide to Pilgrimage*

Pantheon
The Irish

Pantheon
The Irish

Morgan Daimler

MOON
BOOKS
London, UK
Washington, DC, USA

CollectiveInk

First published by Moon Books, 2025
Moon Books is an imprint of Collective Ink Ltd.,
Unit 11, Shepperton House, 89 Shepperton Road, London, N1 3DF
office@collectiveinkbooks.com
www.collectiveinkbooks.com
www.moon-books.net

For distributor details and how to order please visit the 'Ordering' section on our website.

ISBN: 978 1 80341 649 6
978 1 80341 648 9 (ebook)
Library of Congress Control Number: 2024943608

A CIP catalogue record for this book is available from the British Library.

Design: Lapiz Digital Services

UK: Printed and bound by CPI Group (UK) Ltd, Croydon, CR0 4YY
US: Printed and bound by Thomson-Shore, 7300 West Joy Road, Dexter, MI 48130

We operate a distinctive and ethical publishing philosophy in
all areas of our business, from our global network of authors to
production and worldwide distribution.

Contents

This book is dedicated to every pagan in Ireland who has worked to keep these beliefs alive and to rebuild an active pagan presence across the island.

I'd like to acknowledge the hard work of Coire Sois, Pagan Life Rights Ireland, and the Irish Pagan School, as well as the many individuals who work tirelessly to draw attention to pagan beliefs in Ireland today.

With special thanks to C Lee Vermeers for help tracking down some particularly pesky sources from the dark days of the late '90s internet.

Author's Note

This book is part of a series from Moon Books which is meant to offer a solid introduction to a specific pantheon and the beliefs around those beings. Each book follows a loose guideline to cover history, belief, and practice; I am modelling this book on my previous work *Pantheon: The Norse* so that it will follow the same structure, which I believe is the easiest way to tackle this subject. Having previously written a book on Irish paganism and on the Irish deities I am striving not to repeat information here, to offer readers a fresh look at things, but there may be some inevitable crossover as certain subjects must be repeated and there are only so many ways to paraphrase the same information. Nonetheless I will try to keep it interesting, and I hope to make this a good entry way for people curious about the Irish pantheon or who want to begin practicing Irish paganism – or anyone who is curious about the subject.

I personally favour using APA citation in my writing and so throughout this book when a source is being cited you will see the name of the author and date of the book in parenthesis after that. This indicates the book that is being paraphrased in that sentence, both for clarity and to allow readers to further research for themselves if they choose to. I have also included endnotes expanding on points that don't fit neatly into the larger text but are important to touch on, as well as a selection of resources in Appendix B.

This book, more so perhaps than others, is a beginning not an ending, offering a glimpse into a much wider more complicated subject. Hopefully it can serve as a solid place to start for those interested in connecting to or learning about Irish pagan beliefs.

Introduction

"Three glories of speech: steadiness, wisdom, brevity."
  — Triads of Ireland

This book is about the Irish pantheon and the system of belief, both historic and modern, related to that pantheon. The historic worship of Irish gods is complex and open to various interpretations because of the nature of the source material we have to draw from. The blunt truth is that we have no surviving pre-Christian written sources and archaeological evidence will always be somewhat open to debate and interpretation. Because of this, different conclusions can be reached using the same sources and there may not be – often isn't – one clear simple answer. As I like to tell people when discussing the subject, the first thing you must embrace when studying Irish paganism is the contradictory nature of much of what we have to work with. Often the more you dig into the topic the less straightforward the material becomes.

There wasn't a single term used for pre-Christian paganism in Ireland and the words that we do find in early Irish texts like gentlidecht and págánach are loan words from Latin. This likely reflects that the pagan Irish didn't have any word for their own religion, nor any need for such a word until after Christianity entered the picture, at which time we have only the terms used by the Christians in relation to indigenous Irish belief. In modern contexts, Irish paganism is understood as the pre-Christian belief found in Ireland and is used both to refer to modern people who worship multiple deities in Ireland as well as people who focus their paganism on Irish gods.

Irish paganism is often conflated with Celtic[1] paganism to a degree that some people treat the two as interchangeable, although they are not. Irish paganism is focused on Irish belief and practice while Celtic paganism would cast a wider net that could include various Celtic cultures and beliefs. This is important to understand at the outset because the confusion of the two has caused some people to assume that non-Irish deities like Cernunnos were found in Ireland, rather than to appreciate that Irish deities and beliefs are distinct from those found elsewhere. This is not a book which will homogenize Celtic cultures into a single entity, but one that is looking exclusively at Irish paganism.

In Part I we will be looking at the history, beliefs, and practices of the pagan Irish and in Part II we will explore who the Irish gods are as well as related spirits that play an important role in the belief system. It is important to have both some basis in the beliefs as well as a solid source for information on the deities and spirits, so both will be given space. Because of that, however, we can only touch on the various Irish gods and spirits; it would be very easy to write entire books just on that topic but this is intended as a simple overview. If you are interested in diving deeper into those topics there will be a list of resources given in Appendix B.

As with any spiritual or religious system, there are a range of beliefs and practices that different people and groups follow. It would be impossible, even in a much longer book, to cover every variation and iteration of Irish paganism that exists now or has existed, so our focus here will be on providing a broad overview. I must also note at the start that both historic and modern beliefs can have controversial interpretations, such as the endless debate about the timing of holidays, and that not everything is agreed on even among scholars. I will do my best to offer the currently accepted theories and when possible, to discuss some of the other options that people put forward, and I will note where these are considered under debate or uncertain. Unfortunately, in many cases we simply have no clear answers and it is up to each individual to decide what makes the most sense to them.

Is Irish Paganism an Open or Closed Practice?

This is a question that might surprise many people who simply assume it must be an open practice, that is that anyone can do whatever they want with it. The answer is a lot more nuanced, however. Irish paganism is based in Irish culture and belief, and one must be connected to and working from that belief or by definition you aren't following Irish paganism but something else. This spirituality is something that anyone may practice regardless of background, but it isn't something that is an open free for all that people can simply take and redefine however they like. This was a huge problem in the past, especially in the 1990s and early 2000s, when non-Irish authors treated Irish myth and belief this way which resulted in some stunningly bad information being put out as 'genuine' Irish material. This happened in large part because of assumptions that Irish material could be taken and used in any way a person wanted, whether or not that was in line with actual historic or living beliefs – and while it's true that there are no paganism police out there that will stop someone from doing this, it is extremely disrespectful to the culture and the spirits to treat it this way.

It might be best to understand Irish paganism as a semi-closed practice, in that it can be followed by people outside the living culture but that to do so from that basis requires actual effort.

Can Anyone Be an Irish Pagan?

As far as I am personally concerned the Irish Paganism I practice, based on my research into the history and mythology of the pagan culture, is profoundly anti-racist, and anti-homophobic. You are welcome to honour the gods with me no matter what your ethnic background, no matter who your ancestors were, and no matter what your sexual orientation or gender identity is.

I've never been subtle with my opinion on this, and anyone who has ever read my other writings should be aware that I'm very strongly against racism or xenophobia in spirituality. I believe that Celtic language-speaking cultures are not genetic but learned, meaning that anyone with enough effort and acceptance from the culture can belong. Modern Ireland, Wales, and Scotland (for some examples) are diverse places and that diversity needs to be appreciated and respected; the idea that a person having a different ethnicity or skin colour being disallowed from so-called Celtic spirituality is, in my opinion, nonsense.

What I see more and more often is people who clearly establish their ancestry or ancestral connection to Ireland in order to justify or explain why they are choosing that path. And to be clear there is nothing wrong with seeking spirituality by looking to where you or your family has come from. However, I encourage people to really think about why they are doing this. Are you seeking to connect to spirituality through the guidance of ancestors? Or are you using ancestry as a way to feel entitled to a spirituality? Is that ancestral connection a stepping stone forward for you, or is it a shortcut to a sense of belonging? Most importantly, do you think that people with no ancestral connection can still follow Irish paganism?

I have seen people ignore 90% of their ancestors in order to focus on a single one, often many generations back, as if having that one ancestor was a key to accessing a spiritual path. and I always wonder, what about the other 90%?

Speaking as someone in the United States we need to – and I mean need to – acknowledge and integrate all of our ancestry and our wider cultural history even if we don't choose to incorporate all of it into our spirituality. This can be a painful and messy process especially as it inevitably means acknowledging the mistakes and pain inflicted by various groups on each other. But we cannot pick and choose here because ignoring one group that we find distasteful to focus on one we like inevitably creates problems for us on deep levels. My own ancestry comes from various groups which killed or oppressed each other over the last several hundred years, but I can only heal that within myself by acknowledging it.

If we do decide to focus in on one specific aspect of our heritage then it's important not to see that genetic connection as a free pass. What makes you an Irish pagan isn't who your great-grandmother was but how much you work to understand the culture and its gods and spirits. Connection to the culture takes effort and a willingness to be open minded and to learn.

I generally don't like to lean on mythology or textual references for these topics because so often they are twisted to support agendas. However, in this case I do want to point out that in Irish mythology – the Lebor Gabala Erenn specifically – when humans first came to Ireland in the form of the Milesians they acknowledged and respected the Irish sovereignty Goddesses despite having their own deities beforehand. There is a scene where the sons of Mil meet each of three sovereignty Goddesses in turn and make deals with them to secure Ireland for themselves. When one of the Milesians, Donn, argues that they should not do this because they have their own gods already, the elements turn against him and he is drowned. After this battle, when the Milesians have secured Ireland, they must make a pact with the Dagda in order for their crops and cows to flourish. All of this says to me that it isn't where you come from or what gods you worshipped before that matters, but whether a person is willing to enter into a relationship with the gods of Ireland. It might also be worth noting that same source positions all people, both human and mythic, as immigrants to Ireland and claims that humans migrated to Ireland from Spain.

Many people seek spirituality by looking to their own heritage and there is nothing wrong with that, but that heritage is not in any way a prerequisite to Irish paganism. There is, and should be, no proof of ancestry required, no judgment based on appearance, no need to justify your interest. The world is an ever-changing place and diversity is a strength, not a weakness. If your ancestral connection does matter to you then seek to nourish and expand that, certainly, but never fall into the trap of seeing it as necessary to who and what you worship in an Irish context.

You don't need a DNA test to be an Irish pagan. You just need a willingness to learn and connect to the specific culture.

Part I

Chapter 1

History – Celtic or Irish?

"Three ornaments of wisdom: abundance of knowledge,
a number of precedents, to employ a good counsel."
                                          – Triads of Ireland

Before we move into an exploration of Irish pagan beliefs and practices we need to start with a look at history and some of the key concepts that influence our understanding of these things. In particular we need to discuss and hopefully clarify the impact and influence of Celtic culture on Ireland and why this term is falling out of favour both in academia and more broadly. This is particularly important because so much of the readily available material that can be found is in the public domain and profoundly out of date, including using terms that are no longer widely accepted.

The history of Irish paganism is unclear and often contested, with different scholars having sometimes antithetical opinions on the matter. For some, Ireland's culture is a patchwork quilt of outside influences, sewn together across centuries, while for others Irish myth and culture contain key, core features that are unique and have survived across millennia. There is and likely will never be any agreement on these issues, so it is up to the reader to decide for themselves. The crux of much of this is whether Ireland is a Celtic culture and how strongly Celtic culture has influenced Ireland across the years. This is important because if Ireland is viewed as Celtic it tends to be treated interchangeably with other Celtic language speaking cultures, while, if it is understood as distinct but sharing a root language it can be appreciated for itself, in the same way that the so-called Romance language cultures can be. Personally,

I tend to favour the latter view but the former is found across many books, especially older sources.

What Is Celtic?

Celtic is a term for a broad collective of related cultures which share linguistic roots and some aspects of art and myth (Koch, 2005). These peoples developed from proto-Celtic groups who came from Indo-European culture from the late Bronze age through the Iron age. Beginning in central Europe in the Bronze age with the proto-Celtic Urnfield culture and developing into the Celtic Hallstatt culture and eventually La Tène culture (Chadwick, 1970). La Tène is the art style most familiar to people as 'Celtic' and the La Tène cultural artifacts were considered stereotypically Celtic by the 19th century (Koch, 2006). The term itself is derived from the Greek Keltoi which is found in writing back to 500 BCE, although the meaning of the term is uncertain (McKone, 2013). It has been widely, and sometimes rather arbitrarily, applied to a range of historic cultures many of which are now extinct and to a selection of modern cultures which share a linguistic root.

It does get quite muddy when sorting through the historic material because what differentiated a continental Celtic culture 2000 years ago from a Germanic one was often nothing more than how they were labelled by the Greeks or Romans writing about them. This is also complicated because the two cultures share deeper historic roots via Indo-European culture as well as sharing territories across time so that there are not necessarily clear lines between them. Because many of these groups were wiped out by the Romans it is now impossible to truly know much about them or which language they spoke. Nonetheless scholars tend to approach the material with understandings based on dividing these groups into two distinct categories, Celtic or Germanic.

Language is a key marker of Celtic culture and one of the main indicators that a culture was Celtic. Celtic languages once flourished across Europe but slowly concentrated in Western Europe and today survive in six modern nations and their diaspora: Ireland, Scotland, Wales, Isle of Man, Cornwall, and Brittany. Additionally, there are some attempts to recreate and revive Gaulish, one of the most well attested historic Celtic languages.

A Celtic Migration?

Across the 20th century it was widely agreed by scholars on the subject that Celtic culture originated in central Europe and one of the primary theories for many years has been that Celtic culture arrived in Ireland via a migration of people. This idea was based on assumptions that the culture was carried by warlike tribal groups who were slowly pushing west from the late Bronze age onwards, bringing their culture with them as they went. This theory also gave rise to the related, now debunked, theory that the idea of fairies was born out of iron wielding invaders settling Celtic territories and driving the bronze-using inhabitants into the hills.[2] The theory of such a migration has been increasingly challenged over the past several decades as DNA studies have failed to show evidence of any massive population moves during that period, or in some cases, at all. The theory today suggests an adoption of culture rather than migration, with Celtic culture being imported in, possibly via trade, and slowly taking hold and replacing the pre-existing one.

Celtic from the West?

A contrasting theory which was originally written about by professor Barry Cunliffe is that Celtic culture originated in the west, with the so-called insular Celts, and was brought eastwards from there. This theory suggests a much earlier origin of Celtic languages along the Atlantic seaboard which then spread inland and were only later written down, providing an explanation for the locations and dating of early Celtic material.

This theory has received mixed receptions but the recent DNA studies that have shown a lack of population movement may support Cunliffe's idea as it contradicts any claims of population migrations into Ireland during that period. Other scholars, like John Koch, have also written articles in support of a Celtic from the West view.

Celtic from France?

A current theory which may be gaining ground is that both previous views were wrong and based on misinterpreting or cherry-picking data and the truth may literally lie in the middle. This idea, suggested in 2020 by Patrick Sims-Williams, is that Celtic culture and language may have originated in what is now France in the 1st century BCE and spread outwards both east and west from there. This theory leans more heavily on linguistic evidence than previous ones did and revises the dating of a distinct Celtic culture forward by centuries.

Ultimately at this point we do not know which theory is correct or if another theory will emerge to better explain the origins and spread of what we call Celtic culture.

Celtic? Or Irish?

Many pagans today conflate Celtic and Irish cultures, believing that the two are interchangeable when in truth they are largely different. Despite the popular claims to the contrary, there isn't and has never been a single unified Celtic culture, Celtic belief system, or Celtic pantheon. There has been a lot of confusion caused by this misunderstanding, particularly creating an idea that all Celtic gods would have been found in Ireland and that any religious practice found in any Celtic country would also have existed in Ireland; the actual evidence contradicts this. While there are a small number of pan-Celtic deities found across several Celtic nations, the gods of Ireland are largely distinct and even the ones that are shared have unique features and stories in Ireland.

Irish culture may be considered one of the historic and modern Celtic cultures but it is only one of many and there are aspects of Irish pagan belief that are different from those found in other Celtic cultures, sometimes strongly different. These distinctions come from centuries or even possibly millennia of each culture developing individually, and while trade and various interactions may have contributed to some shared features, each culture is also markedly its own. I would encourage readers to view Irish culture as distinct from both other Celtic cultures and the wider concept of 'Celtic' and not muddy the waters with the Celtic label.

Conversion to Christianity

The period of conversion to Christianity in Europe is known to be a bloody one, but Ireland is a notable exception to this. Conversion in Ireland was a slow process and was not marked with violence or with massive social upheaval as was seen elsewhere. Christians established a presence in Ireland by the end of the 4th century and by the 5th century the Pope had sent bishops to the island, including Palladius in 429 CE (Ó hÓgáin, 1999). At this point in the early 5th century Ireland already had a small but settled Christian population complete with churches, monasteries, priests and then bishops (Ó hÓgáin, 1999). This population lived side by side with the pagans of the time, and it wasn't until Patrick's arrival (after Palladius) that evangelism became an issue. Even then Patrick had limited success, was accused of taking bribes, imprisoned, and nearly killed; the Christian church was simply not a significant force in Ireland at this point and the pagans of the time, who were in power, didn't and wouldn't tolerate excessive pushback against their ways (Da Silva, 2006). It would take Ireland several hundred years to fully convert, and the 7th century law codes continued to include druids, although at a reduced rank which showed their lowered esteem, demonstrating that paganism lingered on. This slow conversion may also be indicated by the amount of pagan material preserved in later manuscripts, which were given a veneer of Christianity but included many elements that were clearly Irish.

Irish History and Paganism

A final note as we wrap up this chapter: It is beyond the purview of this book to dive deeply into the complexity of Ireland's history, including the full story of the conversion to Christianity, various invasions, and the period where Ireland was – in some places still is – a colony of England. This would require a book in itself, and indeed many good books on this topic have been written. However, an understanding of these things, especially the impact of colonization on Irish culture, is essential to a wider understanding of every aspect of Irish paganism. I strongly encourage people to dig further into this on their own.

Chapter 2

Mythology

"Three things that constitute a blacksmith: Nethin's spit, the cooking-hearth of the Morrigan, the Dagda's anvil."

— *Triads of Ireland*

Irish mythology is a complex topic, in part because everything we have on the subject was recorded by Christians and we have no existing material that comes from the pagan period. This has resulted in two antithetical approaches to understanding Irish myth: nativism which sees recorded material as containing genuine pagan material to varying degrees, and anti-nativism which sees all surviving material as effectively foreign or influenced by foreign myths and classical stories. I am, myself, nativist in my views which effects my work here and should be understood as my personal bias as I write. I believe that all the myths we have contain at least a seed of actual pagan belief, but it's important to go forward in this section understanding that not everyone shares that view, including some scholars whose work I reference in this book.

There are four main sources for our knowledge of Irish myth today – manuscripts, retellings, folklore, and modern stories – and these will be discussed here, so that readers are familiar with them and what they can tell us. Each source has its own value and no one kind of source should be looked at exclusively; only by taking them all together can a full picture of Irish pagan belief be formed.

Manuscripts – the main source that we have for Irish mythology are the manuscripts, which date from roughly the 9th through

17th centuries. The manuscript sources are not cohesive, nor where they meant to be, and represent a conglomerate of regional beliefs that were cobbled together by the people recording them, as well as later concepts and ideas around mythic beings. Many of the stories found in manuscripts exist in multiple versions and some versions contradict each other; for example, in the Táin Bó Cúailgne there are versions where the Morrigan drives the action while in others its Badb. In the same way, in the Lebor Gabala Erenn, in different versions we see the same set of three sons attributed to the Morrigan, Danu, and Brighid. Things like this aren't errors and they don't indicate that all of these beings were seen as interchangeable, rather this shows that in different areas of Ireland certain beings were more prominent and were then given the significant role in a story.

The manuscripts also often reflect the political climate of the time, focused through the lens of these stories. So, for example, the Cath Maige Tuired tells the story of the Tuatha Dé Danann overthrowing the Fomorians who are oppressing them, describing the Tuatha Dé as a cohesive fighting group led by a noble king, while the Oidheadh Chloinne Tuireann, recorded in the 16th century, describes the same event but with the Tuatha Dé as hesitant and their king, Nuada, as unwilling to challenge the Fomorians until Lugh shames him into doing so, possibly a criticism of Irish society of the time which was suffering under English rule (Williams, 2016).

Manuscripts that touch on the Irish gods or paganism would include:

- The Lebor Gabala Erenn. The Takings of Ireland, a series of tales which appear in multiple versions, or recensions, and describe the settling of Ireland by five waves of mythic beings ending with the arrival of humans.

- The Cét-Cath Maige Tuired. The First Battle of the Plain of Pillars, a story of the arrival of the Tuatha Dé Danann in Ireland and their fight against the Fir Bolg, a previous group of settlers, to gain the island.
- The Cath Maige Tuired. The Battle of the Plain of Pillars, which tells of the Tuatha Dé Danann fighting to overthrow the Fomorians who were oppressing them. Probably the most important of tale of the gods, it exists today in a single preserved manuscript.
- The Dindshenchas – Place Name Stories, a collection of prose and poetic pieces which tell stories of specific places across Ireland, often tying myth to physical locations.
- The Banshenchus. Tales of Women, a collection of information about various mythic, pseudo-historic, and historic women, including an array of goddesses.

There are several distinct cycles in Irish myth including: The Mythic Cycle, Ulster Cycle, Fenian Cycle, the cycle of Kings, and Imramma. Of these the mythic cycle is the most obviously important to Irish pagans, although many of the others also include stories of the gods or spirits.

Retellings – Retellings are myths and folk stories which are taken from their sources and rewritten usually for a slightly different audience who may not have access to the original. Lady Gregory's book *Gods and Fighting Men* or Peter Berresford Ellis's *Celtic Mythology* are retellings which blend together multiple versions of stories into a single version; this blending can cause problems as it usually means leaving out material found in the originals or adding material in written by the author to make the story flow. While there are very good retellings of the myths – Cross & Slover's *Ancient Irish Tales* being a prime example – retellings are not always done well and sometimes contribute to confusion, especially when people are looking to retellings as their main sources rather than the older mythology. On the other hand, retellings can bring the stories to a wider audience and increase accessibility.

Folklore – Folklore generally is the set of beliefs and practices around a subject; folklore in this case is the wider body of stories told within Irish culture about the Tuatha Dé Danann and Aos Sidhe.[3] There is folklore about the Irish gods and spirits outside Irish culture which may be worth considering but it is important to understand the differences between the sources – for example, Irish folklore and Irish-American folklore are not the same thing, despite sharing some beliefs and practices. When seeking to understand Irish paganism its always best to start in Ireland and only move outwards when and where it makes sense, and to understand that some of the folk beliefs outside Ireland may directly contradict those within it, particularly ideas that have been shaped by popular pagan writers of the late 20th and early 21st centuries.

Folklore around the Tuatha Dé Danann often recasts these beings from gods into fairy kings and queens, and sometimes into human characters. Turning a mythic being into a human is something called euhemerization and it is quite common, as stories continue to be told within cultures over time and those cultures shift to a more monotheistic view. This is why you will find folk tales of named beings who appear as gods in the manuscripts where that same being is now described as a human hero. This later view shouldn't be confused for a genuine earlier belief, however.

Modern Stories – the final category here are modern stories, which includes both stories created now that are set in the past as well as stories set today. These may reflect current understandings of deities and beings like the Aos Sidhe, recent anecdotes, as well as creative fiction intended to offer insight into these beings. Popular culture fiction, including various novels as well as role playing games, has had a profound impact on modern pagan belief which has impacted Irish paganism due to the widespread popularity of Irish folklore and myth.

Chapter 3

Cosmology

"Three dead ones that are paid for with living things: an apple-tree, a hazel-bush, a sacred grove."
— Triads of Ireland

There is no single clear source for cosmology within Irish belief and what we do have has often been pieced together from older sources recorded by Christians. This complicates attempts to understand Irish cosmology and is why there are various different understandings of these concepts. What will be discussed in this chapter will be the most widely agreed on ideas and concepts that are found across mythology and into folklore, as well as some modern concepts that are widespread. We will also take a look at some of the key information that is missing from Irish pagan cosmology.

The Otherworld

One key cosmological aspect that we find shared across a range of beliefs so strongly that it is simply presupposed in most stories is the existence of an Saol Eile, the Otherworld, a place that is adjacent to but distinct from the human world. This is the world of the sidhe and, eventually, of the Tuatha Dé Danann. It can be accessed or reached in a variety of ways, sometimes simply by wandering into it unawares and sometimes by intentional travel. It exists within the fairy mounds (sidhe), in magical islands in the west, within certain lakes, and connected to crann sidhe, fairy trees. The understanding of the Otherworld has changed across time but broadly it is a place very much like earth but more inherently magical, with terrain and settlements like the human world but with a variety of different beings living in it, from monsters to the Aos Sidhe.[4] The Otherworld also sometimes includes the human dead or living humans who were stolen away by the Aos Sidhe, as well as some animals like cattle who were taken. It is a place that by some accounts is exceptionally peaceful and bountiful, while other stories describe it as having the same fighting and seasonal cycles as earth, although on different scales.

Sacred Space

The concept of sacred space in Irish paganism is slightly different than what is often found elsewhere, in that all space is seen as having significance and there is a less concrete line dividing the sacred from the profane. Spaces can be blessed or given extra energy by circling them clockwise or sunwise, especially three times, and can be cursed or filled with negative energy by circling them counter clockwise. There is also a deeply embedded idea of 'thin places' or places which are less grounded in this world and closer to the Otherworld and therefore may be seen as especially sacred. Rivers may be associated with specific goddesses, many wells are seen as especially important and connected to healing, and bodies of water in general may be seen as closer to both deities and the Otherworld.

Directions, Realms, Elements, and Energy Centres

When we look at older sources, we find many stories that feature the Otherworld in contrast to the human world but we find less information about more esoteric approaches to cosmology, including sacred directions, elements, different realms, or energy centres within the body. Many of these do exist in more modern forms of Irish paganisms, however, often pieced together from hints in the older sources or poetry so we will consider them here as they somewhat overlap with each other in concept.

Directions – Many forms of paganism around the world include concepts about the sacredness or values of specific directions. The most familiar of these may be the four-direction system of north/earth, east/air, south/fire, west/water common across neopaganism and western witchcraft. We don't have any firm evidence of this in Irish sources, beyond the ingrained idea that moving with the sun (clockwise) was positive and moving against the sun (counterclockwise) was banishing or negative, however, there are some hints that allow us to create a modern structure. The Suidigid Tellaich Temra gives us this directional breakdown based on the locations of the five ancient provinces: *"In the west knowledge, in the north battle, in the east blossoming, in the south melody, in the centre sovereignty"*. From this we can extrapolate a five-direction system including centre.

An alternate four directional system may be used based on the Tuatha Dé Danand na Set Soim, a text which describes the origin of the Tuatha Dé Danann in four potentially Otherworldly[5] cities: Murias, Gorias, Falias, and Findias. Each city is in turn associated with a specific sage or wizard and with one of the four treasures of the Tuatha Dé Danann. None are given directional assignments in the source material but such systems can be created based on associations with the treasures or descriptions of the sages.

- Murias was the home of Semiath, described as a 'fortress of peaks' and was the source of the Dagda's inexhaustible cauldron.
- Gorias was the home of Esrus 'of keen desires' and the source of the sword from which no one could escape, possession of Nuada.
- Findias was the home of Uscais, the 'fair seer', source of the spear of Lugh which no battle could be sustained against.

- Falias was the home of the poet Morfis and source of the only treasure with no set owner, the Lia Fail, a stone which would cry out[6] under every rightful king of Ireland.

Realms – Many modern Irish pagans work with a system of three realms which can be understood roughly as land, sea, and sky, or human world, chthonic world, and celestial world. This isn't universally done but it's fairly common, based in the idea that the number three was particularly important and that an understanding of reality would have incorporated this number and a multi-realm structure as we find in other cultures. For some this understanding breaks down to a realm for the human dead/Aos Sidhe, a realm for living humans, and a realm for the gods, while others place the Aos sidhe with the gods instead of the human dead.

Elements – Most neopagans use a four-element system aligned with the four-directions; however, this is different in Irish paganism. Some use a three-element system, water, earth, and air, to work with the three realms of land, sea, and sky. Others have innovated a five-element system for five directions including centre, and there is also a nine-element system which aligns the human bodyto natural elements to directions:

North – stone – bones
Beneath – earth – flesh
Outwards – plants – hair
West – sea – blood
East – wind – breath
Inwards – moon – mind
South – sun – face
Through – cloud – brain
Above – heaven – head
(O'Dubhain, 1997)

Energy Centres – Interlocked with all of these previous ideas and drawing on outside concepts, most notably the idea of chakras, there are also those who believe that the human body has three main energy centres. This idea draws on a medieval poem known in English as 'The Cauldron of Poesy' which describes three cauldrons that exist in all humans from birth. Although likely metaphors for poetic creativity the three cauldrons have been taken and used as a basis for understanding the flow of energy in the body for many years.

The poem states that not everyone is given the same knowledge or ability, and describes the cauldrons in three positions – upright, sideways, or inverted. The Cauldron of Incubation is upright at birth and gives people wisdom, the Cauldron of Motion is on its side initially, and the Cauldron of Wisdom begins upside down; the second two can be moved to an upright position through effort, learning, or experiencing 'sorrow or joy' (Laurie, 1999). Erynn Rowan Laurie, in the 1999 article 'The Cauldron of Poesy', locates each cauldron within the physical body, with the Cauldron of Incubation in the abdomen, the Cauldron of Motion in the chest, and the Cauldron of Wisdom in the head. It is from this that the concept can be further extrapolated out into energy centres of the body and approached as one might within other systems, although the source material is describing the Cauldrons as sources of poetic wisdom and ability specifically.

Creation

Those interested in Irish paganism are often surprised to learn that we have no preserved creation story. The closest we may come to that are the series of invasions retold in the Lebor Gabala Erenn, although that text presupposes the existence of Ireland at the beginning.[7] We do have some hints of possible creation tales within other stories where we see mythic figures, usually goddesses, creating various pieces of the landscape. In many of these tales, such as those of Tailtiu or Macha wife of Nemed, the goddess struggles to clear the wilderness for cultivation then dies from the effort, which may represent an echo of a now lost cosmogonical story. It is the theme in some creation stories for the deity who creates the world to die in the process. In other stories, like those around the Cailleach, the deity creates the landscape by dropping stones as they pass by. All of these earth shaping stories would seem to echo older creation myths wherein the deity shaped not only that particular area of land but the entirety of creation.

There have been several modern attempts to fill the need for a creation tale. Ella Young, an early 20th century author, wrote a story which placed Brighid as the key figure in the earth's creation and settling. Peter Berresford Ellis in the late 20th century wrote a creation story that placed Danu and Bile[8] as the creators of the earth and the Dagda and Brighid[9] as the forces which created the gods. Alexei Kondratiev also penned a creation myth, placing Danu and Bile as the primordial creators of the world. Each of these attempts involves creative fiction and reworking of known mythology in ways that inevitably make some drastic changes.

Eschatology

Just as we have no creation story, we have no surviving end of the world tale either. The closest we may find is the Morrigan's second prophesy in the Cath Maige Tuired, wherein the Morrigan predicts the end of the world by describing a vision of a world that has fallen into chaos and dishonour. Unfortunately, that prophecy ends abruptly midway and is also quite possibly a later Christian insertion into the older tale and I'd caution people to take it with the proverbial grain of salt.

Ultimately, the Irish understanding of the world may have been closer to preserved accounts of Gaulish beliefs, which claimed that time was cyclical with the world ending and beginning over and over again. This belief is also found to a degree in the less closely related Norse pagan beliefs of the world ending and beginning anew. While this isn't conclusive evidence of anything it may provide at least a hint into the possible older pagan beliefs.

Fate

Dán is an Irish word that translates as "fate" and also as gift, offering, craft, calling, and poem (O Donaill, 1977). It is a complex term but is often understood as the fate or destiny that a person is born with and which is inextricably woven into their life. There is a saying that goes "*A man won't drown whose dán is to hang*" that illustrates this idea that dán is inexorable and inescapable, as does this quote from the Fragmentary Annals: "*We will have whatever our gods and our fate bring us*". This doesn't contradict the concept of free will – we all make our own choices throughout life – but reflects the idea that while some aspects of our life may be flexible others are fixed points. This term closely resembles the Greek idea of fate as something created for each person by a supernatural power, although the Irish appear to have lacked the personification aspect of fate seen in the Greek.

The Soul

A person's soul was believed to reside in their head, which was also the seat of personal power (O hOgáin, 1999). The heads of enemies would be taken with the belief that the owner of such a trophy would also possess the power of the person whose head was taken; in some cases the head would be preserved, usually with oil, or else hung up for all to see as a trophy (Ross, 1998). This is a recurrent motif across Irish mythology, and was so significant that we even see the severed heads of warriors referred to as the goddess Macha's nut crop in the Sanas Cormaic.

The soul was also seen as immortal, passing from life to life and form to form in several stories, persisting in a non-corporeal form in later folklore, or travelling on to a different reality or spiritual destination. In the Tochmarc Etaine Etain is transformed from one of the Tuatha Dé Danann into the shape of a bug, then reborn in a human form when that bug is drunk by a woman. Similarly, the two fairy swineherds in the De Choppur in Dá Muccida live lives in a range of animal forms before finally becoming small insects who are drunk by cows after which they are reborn as bulls.

The Afterlife

Afterlife beliefs in Irish paganism are, unsurprisingly, complex and vary between groups and traditions. There is no single belief that is shared, except that the soul itself is eternal. This is reflected in the idea that the soul continues on in some way; embedded in the oldest myths and into modern belief we find no concepts of either a place of eternal reward or of eternal punishment. This continuation of the soul forms the basis of the afterlife beliefs across different sources.

So, let's look at some of the more commonly held beliefs about the afterlife that you will find.

Reincarnation – This is not overt in stories but is present across various myths where specific named characters are seen going through multiple lives and forms as discussed in the previous section. Unlike some other views of reincarnation, a soul doesn't always remain in a human form, however, and we see stories of beings passing through a variety of animal and humanoid lives. Although not discussed as a general concept applying to all souls it is at the least implied as possible.

Several different Irish myths discuss the topic of the reincarnating soul including the story of Tuan mac Cairill in the Lebor na hUidre. In this story Tuan mac Cairill tells the tale of

Ireland from the beginning, which he has witnessed throughout his various lives as a man, then as a stag, a wild boar, an eagle, a salmon, and then a man again. As he says in the story:

> My name is Tuan son of Carell. But once I was called Tuan son of Starn, son of Sera, and my father, Starn, was the brother of Partholan.

In one version of the conception tale of Cu Chulainn, a baby is born to woman in a fairy mound, only to die and then be reconceived by the king's sister Dechtire and reborn as her son Setanta (later known as Cu Chulainn).

The Otherworld – From stories we find in folklore, and even depending on how we choose to view stories like that of Oisín and Niamh, a person may join the fairies (the Daoine Sidhe) usually after being taken by them. This may not be a universal fate shared by everyone, however there are those Irish pagans who believe that the land of the human dead is a part of the Otherworld and that human dead may abide there, at least until their soul may be reborn (O'Brien, 2005).

Tech Duinn – The House of Donn, the first human to die in Ireland and the primordial ancestor or God of the Dead, is said in some stories to be the destination of all souls. According to the Lebor Gabala Erenn "The grave-mound of every man is there." And the Dindshenchas tells us that pagan souls must visit Donn after death to pay their respects to him before moving on, while Christian souls only view Tech Duinn from a distance but still must pass near it and see it before going to heaven. Both of these accounts make Tech Duinn at the least a place that all souls of the dead must pass through.

Remaining Earthbound – It is also possible when a person dies that their spirit may wander on Earth as Irish folklore has an abundance of wandering souls to be found. This speaks to the permanence of the soul and the ability of the dead and living to interact, something that appears in tales for the Echtra Nera to modern anecdotes.

Chapter 4

Ritual

*"Three maidens that bring love to good fortune: silence,
diligence, sincerity."*

– Triads of Ireland

Irish pagan rituals, like most pagan rituals, can be very diverse.
Here we are going to look at an overview of some common
themes and concepts that are found in historic and modern
rituals to give an idea of how the subject would be approached.
Exactly how these pieces are put together and implemented
today depends on the individual or group.

Direction

One thing that is found across various sources is the concept
of entering a sacred place or space, especially for ritual or
magical purposes, by first walking three times around the space
sunwise [clockwise]. This practice has remained through the
modern period in folk practices, but the concept of approaching
somewhere from a sunwise direction with positive intentions,
or indeed circling it against the sun for cursing, can be found
in the mythology indicating the deep roots of the idea. It is a
quick and basic way to draw beneficial energy, to simply walk
clockwise around something. This is utilized in ritual as well,
both before it begins and during the ceremony.

Ritual Structure

There is no set structure for rituals in Irish paganism, nor do
we have definitive information about historic practices. It
is likely that a general pattern was followed of demarcating
space, invocations, and ritual offerings, possible followed by

divination, then incorporating some type of communal feast or meal; it is also likely that sacred fire and water played key roles. There is a lot of leeway here for individuals and groups to design their own approaches within this general outline.

My suggestion for an Irish pagan ritual outline would look like this, based on a distillation of the information we do have and later folk practices:

- Circle ritual space or process into it moving clockwise.
- If cleansing[10] is required or desired, burn an appropriate herb or incense.
- Invoke the deities or spirits of the occasion.
- State the purpose of the rite.
- Make appropriate offerings, possibly including clean water, butter, milk, or bread.
- If desired utilize a form of divination to check efficacy of the rite or look forward at the coming season/period of time.
- Express gratitude to the gods and spirits you invoked.
- Adjourn and share a meal, leaving a portion aside for the gods and spirits.

Feasting

Ritual feasting is one aspect of ancient Irish polytheism that is found from mythology through modern practice. It had spiritual overtones, with portions being offered to the gods and spirits, and also served to bring communities together.

Archaeological evidence points to the important role that seasonal ritual feasting played in Iron Age Ireland, specifically through faunal remains at known ritual centers like Dun Ailinne (Koch, 2005). Although it can be difficult to discern from such remains what the context of the animal's use was, generally, in cases where ritual sites are being examined, it is known that the site itself had a ritual purpose based on its design and the deposited bones show evidence of special disposal that is not consistent with ordinary domestic use, particularly wrapping and burial (McCormick, 2010). This hard evidence is supported by references in mythology to the great feasts held at these same sites on notable dates, particularly Samhain and Lúnasa:

> ...and that of every king in Ireland as well, for the purpose of holding Tara's Feast: for a fortnight before samhain that is to say, On samhain-day itself, and for a fortnight after." (Jones, n.d.)
>
> With the men of Ireland too it was general that out of all airts they should resort to Tara in order to the holding of Tara's Feast at samhaintide. For these were the two principal gatherings that they had: Tara's Feast at every samhain (that being the heathens' Easter); and at each Lughnasa, or' Lammas-tide,' the Convention of Taillte. (O'Grady, 1892).

Feasting on the holy days played a vital social role and one that was intrinsically tied to the agricultural calendar. As Nerys Patterson notes in *Cattle Lords and Clansmen* the pagan festival dates survived after the religion itself was lost due to their connection to the seasonal turning points and rhythms of domestic animal husbandry (Patterson, 1994). Fergus Kelly in *Early Irish Farming* discusses the increase in value of pigs and cows at specific holy days, including Samhain and Lunasa, indicating both the pivotal nature of these days and their intrinsic relationship to agricultural events (Kelly, 1997). Even as the religious overtones were lost the superstitions and appreciation of the cycles associated with the farming year remained, and these can be appreciated today for the hints they provide of the older pagan beliefs and practices.

Samhain was a period of both feasting and assemblies which especially featured the consumption of young pigs, called 'banb samna'[11] (Kelly, 1997). Faunal remains also indicate that the remains of cattle found at Iron Age ritual sites including Dún Ailinne were those of young cows, rather than of older animals (McCormick, 2010). McCormick in his paper 'Ritual Feasting in Iron Age Ireland' argues persuasively that the feasting which occurred at these times at these ritual sites would have been part of a larger event that included the sacrifice of the animal to the gods being honoured, their preparation, and then consumption by the community, a process which was shared by other contemporary Indo-European cultures.

Evidence suggests that the animals were killed immediately before consumption and then boiled rather than cooked in fire (McCormick, 2010). This could possibly indicate that formal ritual feasts may have often featured stewed dishes. In several myths the broth of a special or ritual meal is given cleansing or initiatory properties that are used to elevate a person's social status or cleanse the person of existing social stigmas, including allowing someone to return from a wild state to a civilized one (McCone, 1990). If such stories are taken as mythic examples of a cultural understanding of the power of ritual food preparation and consumption, combined with faunal evidence of ritual animals being boiled, it is not unreasonable to suppose that eating the meat with a liquid was usual and held significance.

Looking at the total of the evidence it can be concluded that feasting at holy days such as Samhain and Lunasa would primarily have featured meals of pork and beef, likely cooked by boiling, preferably meat from younger animals. In a modern context this can be carried forward with the use of these two types of meat as the centrepiece of rituals feasts. Although many people today cannot or prefer not to raise and butcher their own animals, the aspect of the ritual feast for those who do still choose to eat meat can be kept through the choice of meat used and its preparation. Even for those who do not eat meat this concept can still be used, with a communal meal after ritual occurring for both spiritual and social purposes. A portion of the meal should be set aside to offer to the gods and spirits.

Offerings

Offerings play a key role in both ritual itself as well as general Irish pagan practice. The concept of leaving offerings for the gods and Aos Sidhe is rooted in very old ideas expressed in mythology as well as modern folk beliefs. In De Gabail in t-Sida we are told that after humans arrived in Ireland and the Tuatha Dé Danann went into the sidhe, the cows and crops of Ireland failed, until an agreement was made between the Milesians and the Dagda, king of the Tuatha Dé, that a tithe of the harvest would be given to the gods. This ensured prosperity and established the idea of reciprocal offerings – humans give to the gods and the gods bless the land and animals so they flourish. In a modern folk belief written about in *Festival of Lughnasa* a tithe of the harvest is given to the Aos Sidhe so that they will bless it, echoing the older idea found in myth.

Ancient offerings have been found in bodies of water and bogs, including jewellery, weapons, and butter. There is an older reference to a folk practice involving offering porridge into the earth for the gods, and bread or other food might be left out (Sjoedstedt, 2000; MacNeill, 1962). Offerings to the Aos Sidhe might include milk, butter, or in some cases even blood,[12] left at fairy forts, near fairy trees, or poured onto the ground for them (Evans, 1957; O hOgáin, 1995). In the same way the top portion of alcohol still is seen as the fairies' tithe and in some places the first bit of a drink was spilled onto the ground for the Good Folk, as was the first bit of milk from a milking (Evans-Wentz, 1911). These offerings are seen as giving the gods and spirits their due, an obligation, not as a gift from us to them and that should be kept in mind.

Traditionally offerings were (are) left outside, ideally in an area where they won't immediately be disturbed, and often near an identified liminal place like a fairy tree or fort. In some later folk practices offerings might be left on a window ledge or stone. It was accepted that sometimes animals might consume anything placed out, although folk belief is divided on whether this is fine for the animal or potentially dangerous; the wider belief is that the item itself is not physically taken but the substance or essence of the item is absorbed or removed.

Chapter 5

Celebrations and Prayers

*"Three sounds of increase: the lowing of a cow in milk,
the din of a smithy, the swish of a plough."*
                              – Triads of Ireland

As with any spirituality or religion the celebration of holy days, significant life events, and prayers are important to Irish paganism. In this chapter we will explore the various holidays as well as some important life events and how they were marked, and at the end I will include a few preserved pagan prayers from the older source material. Much of this chapter will focus on evidence of older practices and historic material to give readers a sense of the basis for these concepts in Irish paganism but this should in no way be understood as definitive or reflective of modern practices. Modern Irish paganism is diverse and includes a variety of approaches that have grown out of these older sources and related folk practices.

Holy Days

The timing and celebration of the various holy days is surprisingly contentious, especially for those used to the idea of a firmly set, agreed on schedule of holidays.

In Irish paganism it is generally agreed that the four fire festivals of Samhain, Imbolc, Bealtaine, and Lúnasa are significant holidays, but there is no such agreement about the solstices and equinoxes. This is, in part, because we have a decent amount of evidence around the fire festivals being celebrated historically but less, or none, around the various astronomical dates. It has been suggested by those who do honour those dates that their celebration was subsumed by Christian holy days that are placed close to them, such as Saint John's Day which is near midsummer or Saint Patrick's Day near the spring equinox, but unfortunately there simply isn't enough evidence to prove the theory. Because of this some people do choose to incorporate those dates while others ignore them.

The four fire festivals are less controversial to celebrate, until we look at when they are celebrated. The dating of these holidays is possibly the most consistent and sometimes intense debate to be found in Irish paganism, with people holding various theories with a passion, often insisting their view is the only true one. There are three main theories and one adjacent approach which we will discuss: calendar dates, astrological dates, agrarian timing, and convenience. The calendar dates occur on the first of the month the holiday occurs in, with three of those months – November, May, and August, taking their name in Irish from the respective holiday; despite this the celebration of each holiday usually begins the evening before. The calendar dates are noted in the older written material and have been understood and used for over a millennium at least. In contrast the astrological dates are a newer theory that isn't found in older sources, but one with strong advocates. This theory times the festivals by the astrological midpoint between solstices and equinoxes, usually occurring a few days to a week or so after the calendar dates, and bases the practice on the neolithic sites that are aligned with the festivals. These sites feature a time when a beam of sunlight will illuminate a specific stone either within or as part of the monument itself, such as cairn S at Sliabh na Calleigh which is aligned to Lúnasa (Murphy, 2024). And the idea is that these neolithic sites were created by the indigenous Irish prior to Celtic influence as markers for their holidays, and hence reflect the most accurate date to celebrate. The third theory is that festivals were timed based on agrarian signs because those were the events the festival was marking. So, Samhain was celebrated at the first frost or end of the harvest, Imbolc was celebrated when the ewe's began giving milk or birthing lambs, Bealtaine was when the hawthorn flowers bloomed or alternately when the herds were put out to summer pastures, and Lúnasa occurred when the harvest began in late summer. It is, of course, possible that originally all of these three things, calendar date, neolithic monument alignment, and agrarian signs, would have naturally lined up or overlapped but today there is some variance between them. Finally, the adjacent, and thoroughly modern, approach is to celebrate on the closest date that it is possible to arrange a celebration which is convenient for participants in our very busy world.

Below we will explore some of the history and folk practices associated with the four fire festivals as well as with midsummer, which is the only well attested astronomical celebration.

Samhain

"... that I shall fight without harm to myself from Samuin, i.e., the end of summer. For two divisions were formerly on the year, that is, summer from Beltaine (the first of May), and winter from Samuin to Beltaine." – Tochmarc Emer

Samhain is possibly the most well-known of the Irish pagan holidays, despite being co-opted and merged with Halloween. Historical references mention the first of November, a month named for the holiday in Irish, although it is usually celebrated in folk tradition beginning the night before. Those using astrological timing look for the sun to be at 15 degrees in Scorpio, which is usually around 7th November.

References to this holiday can be found going back 1,000 years in the manuscript material where it was positioned as the turning point of the year from summer to winter and was also a time of upheaval when the Otherworld and the dead were especially close to the human world and able to interact with it. In mythology pivotal events occur at this time, like the battle between the Tuatha Dé Danann and the Fomorians, and several stories take place at this time because of the inherent dangers of it, such as the Echtra Nera where we find the main character interacting with dead men and the Aos Sidhe on Samhain.

The name of the holiday has an uncertain meaning but O'Clery's Irish Glossary, a medieval text, suggests *"samhfhuin .i. fuin an tsamhraidh"* [samhfhuin, that is end of the summer] as its meaning (eDIL, 2024). While this is a folk etymology it has gained a lot of popularity and many people today simply accept this as the definition of the term. Whether or not that is true, it certainly resonates with the timing and purpose of the holiday.

The Genemain Aedh Sláne refers to Samhain as "the pagans' Easter" and claims that a huge feast was held at Teamhair [Tara] every year at that time. It also marked a notable shift from the activities and frenetic pace of summer to the less active and more household-focused period of winter (Patterson, 1994). It was during this slower time that couples would court or families would negotiate marriages, which would usually be completed around mid-February (Patterson, 1994). Samhain then, historically, was a holiday which stood on the hinge of the year and of the social season for humans.

The Otherworld was thought to be especially open and active at Samhain. Several stories, including the aforementioned Echtra Nera, take place on or near Samhain and involve beings of the Otherworld in some way, usually presenting a danger to those who venture out at night. It is on this night that King Ailill Olum first encounters Áine and her father on Cnoc Áine, this time that the battle between the Tuatha Dé and Fomorians is fought and when Óengus finds the mysterious woman of the sidhe who has haunted his dreams, and it is at Samhain that the three headed monster came from Uaimh na gCat, the Cave of Cats in Roscommon, which is called the sidhe of Cruachan It is said that all the sidhe in Ireland opened at Samhain and the Aos

Sidhe moved from their summer homes to their winter homes (Evans, 1957). This is, perhaps, a folklore echo of the mythic idea, presented in the Lebor Gabala Erenn, that the magic which concealed the Aos sidhe and Tuatha Dé Danann from mortal eyes failed during the three days around Samhain. This is a time when the spirits of the Otherworld are more likely to be encountered and caution is needed – as well as respect – in dealing with them. Even through the 20th century, if not today, it is believed that no fruit should be picked after Samhain, as the púca would spit or urinate on anything left in the fields (Evans, 1957).

Bonfires are a long-standing tradition on this holiday, stretching from mythology to today. Sometimes these fires were bone-fires where animal bones would be gathered and burnt with the wood of the fire. Various forms of divination were engaged in, often involving the bonfires, and it's possible that these reflected older magical practices that were slowly changed from actively protective to prognostication (Evans, 1957).

Although modern non-Irish Halloween traditions have spread to Ireland there is also a history of uniquely Irish traditions around this time. In Ireland up until around a hundred years ago there was still a practice in Cork of a small parade led by someone dressed as a white mare that would go from house to house singing and asking for "tolls" (Evans, 1957; Danaher, 1972). In some parts of modern Ireland children still chant "Help the Halloween party! Any apples or nuts?" when trick or treating, perhaps reflecting older traditions (Danaher, 1972).

The human dead also play a role at this time. It was an old practice in Ireland to light a candle for each deceased member of the family and to leave the doors unlocked – in some cases even open – and to leave out either fresh water or porridge as an offering to those ancestors who chose to visit (Evans, 1957;

Danaher, 1972). This was an acknowledgement both that the dead were more present and that it was respectful to welcome them, although it is impossible to know how much this practice may have been influenced by Christian beliefs around All Souls Day.

Imbolc

"To Oimolc, i.e., the beginning of spring, viz., different (ime) is its wet (folc), viz the wet of spring, and the wet of winter. Or, oi-melc, viz., oi, in the language of poetry, is a name for sheep, ... Oi-melc, then, is the time in which the sheep come out and are milked" – Tochmarc Emer

The name of the holiday is, hopefully unsurprisingly, contentious, with no firm agreement on what it means, or even what the name originally was with both Oimelc and Imbolc in contention. The most popular theory draws on an old Irish glossary entry, echoed in the Tochmarc Emer quoted above, which claims the name Oimelc is a compound from words for ewe and milk, connecting the holiday to the time period where lambs are born. Imbolc is suggested to have come from imb-bolg, in bag, also referencing the sheep being in milk. In older Irish translations the word is simply glossed with Candlemas as the two holidays overlapped. For our purposes we will be using the more popular name of Imbolc, although it should be noted that Oimelc is a valid alternative.

The dating of Imbolc has also become somewhat complicated, as the oldest references would put it on the first of February, with celebration beginning the night before, but conflation with Candlemas on 2nd February has caused some to celebrate Imbolc the night of the 1st into the day of the 2nd. Meanwhile those following astrological timing might aim for the sun being in 15 degrees Aquarius around roughly the 5th.

Of the four Irish fire festivals Imbolc is the most family oriented, although it does also have wider community aspects. While we don't have any surviving information about the ancient ways that this day was celebrated, we do have a plethora of folk traditions to draw on, with the role of saint Brigit and the pagan Goddess Brighid often blurred and easily shifted fully into paganism. With some slight alteration all of these traditions can be celebrated by any pagan family to honour Imbolc and the holiday's main deity, Brighid.

A basic overview of the Irish traditions, most of which were actively practiced into the 20th century, is helpful in giving the reader both an understanding of the holiday and of ways that it can be adapted for modern family practice. There were often regional variations in practice and even in the tone of the celebrations, from solemn to comical, which created a wide array of different traditions associated with this holiday (Danaher, 1972). Generally, it was the daughters of the household who played the main roles, although the mother might also be called to do so if there were no daughters. This is in contrast to other traditions which place the father as the main actor in any rituals, divination, or prayers, and establish the more domestic tone of Imbolc. The prominence of women and daughters also demonstrates the importance placed on Brighid at this holiday, with the women and girls often being the main intercessors between Brighid and the family in the ritual enacted or playing the role of Brighid herself. Imbolc also places a strong emphasis on children's participation that is lacking at other holidays which tend to have a more adult tone.

Weaving new Brighid's crosses – symbols of protection, health, and blessing – was an important Imbolc tradition in many places. One ritual that was enacted in Connaught, Sligo, Leitrim, Mayo, Roscommon, and Ulster before the Brighid's crosses were woven for the new year on the eve of the festival was for the eldest daughter to take the part of Brighid and wait outside carrying the material for the project (Danaher, 1972). She would then knock three times, proclaiming herself to be Brighid requesting entrance; she is warmly welcomed in and the family sits down to dinner with an elaborate blessing prayer (Danaher, 1972). The meal often prominently featured dairy products, and if the family was wealthy might also include fresh mutton (Danaher, 1972). After eating the meal, the family would sit and weave the new crosses, with the largest sprinkled with water and hung up on the wall until the next Imbolc (Danaher, 1972). In parts of Leitrim there was also a children's practice to use a small rectangle of wood and with potato paste attach peeled rushes in shapes symbolizing the moon, sun, and stars which would be hung up alongside the woven crosses (Danaher, 1972).

Another tradition was to create an effigy or doll, called a Brideog [little Brighid], representing Brighid. The Brideog might be made of straw from the last sheaf of the harvest, leftover rushes from weaving the crosses, a re-purposed child's doll, or the dash from the butter churn. The effigy would be decorated with a white dress and mask or carved turnip, and might be comical, grotesque, or beautiful in appearance (Danaher, 1972). In some parts of Ireland, the Brideog was carefully and elaborately decorated with shells, crystals, and other natural adornments (Carmichael, 1900). In some places, including Ulster, Connaught, Leinster and Munster, the children would process from house to house carrying the Brideog and pronouncing Brighid's blessing on each home (Danaher, 1972). At each home the people give gifts to the effigy, and the mother of the household gives food to the children in the procession, usually cheese, butter, or bread; this food would later be used by the children for a feast of their own (Carmichael, 1900). In other areas including Cork, Clare, Galway, Mayo, and Kildare a Brideog might not be used but, rather, the unmarried girls would form the procession with one of their number chosen to represent Brighid (Danaher,

1972). In Ulster it was said that the chosen girl wore a crown of rushes, called a crothán Brighite, and carried a shield (sgaith Bhrighite) on her arm; she carried Brighid's crosses to hand out telling each household that it was the sword of Brighid (Danaher, 1972). In other areas the procession might collect food from each house, and in some cases might be comprised entirely of men or boys who would play music at each house (Danaher, 1972). In these cases, the procession was often referred to as 'Biddy Boys' (Evans, 1957).

On the eve of Imbolc, in those homes that used an effigy as a Brideog, a small bed would be prepared, made of rushes or of birch twigs (Estyn Evans, 1957). In some cases, the older women in the home would prepare or shape a small cradle, the leaba Bride or bed of Brighid, for the effigy to sleep in (Carmichael, 1900). In this tradition the effigy is made with great care and a ritual is enacted, much like the one mentioned earlier with the reeds for the crosses, where the effigy is taken outside and invited in. In one tradition the women of the house prepare everything and then one goes and stands in the open door, bracing on the door jambs, and loudly invites Brighid in three times, telling her that her bed is ready (Carmichael, 1900). The Brideog is placed in the bed with a small wand, the slat Brighid, which may be made of birch, hazel, willow or another white wood (Carmichael, 1900).

Another common Imbolc practice was the blessing of a brat Brighid [Brighid's cloak] a piece of cloth that would be left out overnight with the belief that Brighid would pass by and bless it with healing qualities. The cloth would be safely kept throughout the year and was thought to be an especially potent cure for headaches. In some areas of south western Ireland spinning, milling, or any work that would mean turning a wheel was not allowed on Imbolc (Danaher, 1972). A generally festive air existed around this holiday and every household, whatever their means, would have at least one special dish served at dinner to mark the occasion; it was usual to place a cake or piece of buttered bread on an outside window sill as on offering to Brighid (Danaher, 1972).

Bealtaine

"To Beldine, i.e. Beltine, viz., a favouring fire. For the druids used to make two fires with great incantations, and to drive the cattle between them against the plagues, every year." – Tochmarc Emer

Bealtaine is mentioned in older sources happening on the 1st of May, although celebrations would begin the evening before, and the Irish name for the month comes from this holiday. In folk traditions it was not so much a single day's event as something that occurred across three days or so, but with a focus on one main day, further muddying the waters around timing. Those who follow an astrological system would aim for the sun being at 15 degrees in Taurus, roughly around 5th May. Those who time by agrarian signs look for the hawthorn to bloom or wait until we are safe from any risk of frost.

Bealtaine is sometimes also called May Day and an older name for it may be Cétshamain "first Samain" although the context is uncertain and scholars do not agree on its meaning or significance. Bealtaine itself is also of uncertain meaning with 'opening fires', 'lucky fires', and 'bright fires' all having been suggested as possibilities. The Sanas Cormaic, an early Irish glossary suggested a connection between the name and the Biblical deity Ba'al but that is considered spurious now and disregarded. The second part of the name, taine from older Irish tene, is inarguably fire but the beginning portion of the name is where the uncertainty lies as it can be read several different ways, complicated by the non-standard orthographic nature of older Irish.

Bealtaine stood opposite Samhain on the calendar and in many ways represented opposite themes; where Samhain was a time of harvest and of the Dead, Bealtaine was a time of blessing and planting (McNeill, 1959). It was on Bealtaine that the herds were sent out to their summer pastures, and in the old stories it was on Bealtaine that many important events occurred such as the Tuatha Dé Danann first arriving in Ireland. It is said that in ancient Ireland all fires were put out on the eve of Bealtaine and then the Druids would light a sacred fire at Tara which would be passed from hilltop to hilltop and home to home until all the fires were re-lit. (Wilde, 1991). Bealtaine is the beginning of summer and was the time that contracts were renewed, herds moved, and crops planted.

The Aos Sidhe were thought to be especially active and powerful on Bealtaine, and in some sources for the first three days of May. As with Samhain it was on Bealtaine eve that the Aos Sidhe moved from one hill to another, and being more active were most likely to steal children or cause mischief (Danaher, 1972). Caution was needed to guard against them stealing the household's luck, dairy products, or herbs, and the best protection against this was strewing primroses across the threshold (Wilde, 1991). This belief also meant that strangers were looked on with great suspicion, lest they actually be Aos Sidhe in disguise, and there were strong prohibitions against giving away or lending milk or fire on Bealtaine. Offerings of food might be made to appease the Daoine Maithe, or else a bit of iron or Rowan would be carried as protection. (Danaher, 1972).

In Ireland up to fairly recent times, bonfires were a large public affair that occurred the night before or on the night of Bealtaine, although the practices are dying out today. These fires were traditionally true bonfires, or "bone-fires", made with a mix of wood and the bones of cows and horses as well as the horns of cows (Evans, 1957). The fires would be built in open public spaces and the people would gather, whether or not they had celebrated earlier, and drink and sing around the fire (Danaher, 1972). It seems that originally the bonfire traditions were common in every town and village but over time slowly died out in many areas. In modern folk practice the bonfires would be jumped over to increase a person's fertility and show their bravery (Evans, 1957). In earlier times the fire would have been built in two halves and the livestock driven through, as well as the ash from the Bealtaine fire used to bless the fields. (Danaher, 1972). Driving the cattle and sheep between the Bealtaine fires goes back at least a thousand years in practice and is referenced in the oldest glossaries, the belief apparently being that doing this would bless and protect the herds in the summer pastures.

Both fire and water were used for blessing and as the bonfires were created to bless the herds and people, so too was water collected for blessing. Holy wells might be visited, with due ceremony, and the person might wash in the well or take a small amount of water home with them. In Ireland, the first water drawn from a well, called "the top of the well" or "the luck of the well", was believed to be especially powerful for either good or bad intent (Danaher, 1972). Another practice was the collection of the dew on Bealtaine morning, as it was believed that this water had special healing and blessing properties. It might be gathered with a rope or piece of cloth, and some folk accounts mention stealing this dew from neighbours as a way to take their luck for the year.

In Ireland, the Rowan is believed to be the best of all protections against bad luck and enchantment so on May Day morning a branch of Rowan might be woven into the ceiling to protect the house and all within it for the next year (Danaher, 1972). One ceremony noted from Laois called for the head of the family to light a candle and bless the door, hearth, and the four corners of the home, as well as each family member from oldest to youngest, and then the area around the home where a rowan branch should be placed. (Danaher, 1972). More generally rowan might also be hung above doorways, tied to the horns or cattle, or shaped into a cross above a door for protection.

It has been the custom for the children to gather flowers on May eve, possibly a holdover of the people once going out before dawn on May morning; these flowers were then hung up or strewn around the home for luck (Danaher, 1972). On Bealtaine itself, flowers were tied to the bridles of horses and the horns of cows for the same purpose (Danaher, 1972). Flowers were also gathered and used to decorate wells, in order to bless and protect them (Evans, 1957). In Munster, a selection of wood boughs were gathered, generally of Holly, Hazel, Elder, Rowan, and Ash, while in Munster it was Sycamore (Danaher, 1972). In contrast, however, the boughs from fairy trees like Blackthorn and Hawthorn[13] were seen as extremely unlucky in one area but might be lucky in another, however, the general belief was not to disturb the fairy trees or to bring these boughs into the home.

Any herbs gathered on Bealtaine were believed to be especially potent. Yarrow, an herb already believed to be good for nearly anything, was seen as being ideal if gathered on Bealtaine (Wilde, 1991). No herb, however, could be gathered with an iron knife because the iron would ruin any magical properties held by the plant. Plants gathered on May Day were ideally gathered at dawn with the dew still on them, as the dew itself also imparted a blessing (Wilde, 1991). All charms and magics were most powerful on Bealtaine so it was also believed to be a time when witches were most active (Danaher, 1972; Wilde 1991).

Another Irish custom was the preparation of a female effigy, called the "May Baby" that was bedecked with flowers and paraded around the town or village; some theorize that this is an older pagan element related to honouring a goddess (Danaher, 1972). As the May Baby is carried around music is played and a married couple, chosen beforehand, dances in a comically sexual manner around the effigy to entertain it; this procession is believed to grant fertility to the land and the people who observe it and belief in its efficacy was so strong that married women without children were known to travel great distances to receive this blessing (Danaher, 1972). A related practice was the May Boys, a troupe of boys or young men that travelled around singing songs like:

Summer! Summer! The milk of the heifers,
And ourselves brought the summer with us,
The yellow summer, the white daisy,
And ourselves brought the summer with us!

A widespread Irish custom was the placement of a "May bush", a branch or bough of a tree (sometimes a Hawthorn or Holly) that was placed by the front door for luck and decorated with yellow flowers, brightly coloured ribbons, and egg shells (Danaher, 1972). On the night of May Day candles might be lit on or around the bush and people would gather and dance around it; in Ireland, in previous centuries, large parties were held which included feasting and music (Danaher, 1972). The bush itself might be left standing all month, or until the decorations began falling apart, or in some areas was burned in the nighttime bonfire (Danaher, 1972). This practice had begun to die out but has seen a recent surge of revival.

In Ireland divination on Bealtaine focused largely on the weather for the coming growing season. The direction that the wind was blowing on Bealtaine day would indicate whether the summer would be a good one or a bad one, and in some areas snow still visible on Bealtaine was seen as a very bad omen (Danaher, 1972). Another practice was to sweep the threshold clean and then lightly scatter ashes over it; in the morning a footprint coming into the home meant a marriage, while one leaving meant a death in the family in the coming year (Wilde, 1991).

Midsummer and Lá Fhéile Eoin

The only non-Fire Festival that is given significant attention or retains clear remnants of pagan practice is Midsummer, although much of the traditions for it have been moved to Lá Fhéile Eoin on the 24th of June.

The festival, like most other Irish ones, begins on the night before and goes into the next day. Oiche Fhéile Eoin and Lá Fhéile Eoin are celebrations of midsummer, but in many ways, they are similar to and connected to the previous Bealtaine celebrations. The Daoine Maithe were especially active at this time of year and were known to be seen on the sidhe associated with them. Extra precautions were needed to stay safe from their mischief or outright maliciousness on this night. It was also common for prayers to be offered to and for the dead on this night (Danaher, 1972).

There are many traditions associated with Lá Fhéile Eoin [24th June] as well as with the night before, Oiche Fhéile Eoin [23rd June]. There is much supposition that the celebrations of this feast day in the church represent attempts to Christianize earlier pagan midsummer celebrations (Ó Súilleabháin, 1967). Probably the most well-known practice and the one that has survived the longest into the modern era are the bonfires. People from the community would gather and build a bonfire on Oiche Fhéile Eoin, sometimes several, and the herds would be driven through them and the smaller ones jumped over sideways for health, fertility, and luck (Ó hÓgáin, 1995; Danaher, 1972). It was said to be lucky to walk three times sunwise around the bonfire on this night; by some accounts doing this ensures health for the year to come (Ó hÓgáin, 1995; Wilde, 1991). Even the smoke from the fires was lucky and the areas it drifted over were said to have received the same blessing as areas that later received its ash.

The bonfires were community events where people would gather and celebrate together with music and dancing; the fire itself would be built from wood and bones gathered from all the households in the community. At the fire the men would compete with each other in games of skill while the women would pray for good crops and food supply (Danaher, 1972). The belief was strong that to neglect these prayers might result in a failure of the fish to come up river or bring a blight over the crops (Danaher, 1972). The practice of bonfires slowly died out into the mid-20th century but could easily be revived and indeed the celebration seems to be seeing a revival in modern Ireland.

The bonfires also had other, more esoteric uses. Because they were seen as powerful supernatural fires that carried blessings they could be used to safely dispose of magical or holy items that needed to be gotten rid of. Holy items, such as statues or rosary beads, that had been worn out or broken could be thrown into a bonfire on Oiche Fhéile Eoin, and so could magical items that had been used for either blessing or cursing (Danaher, 1972). Charms that had served their purpose as well as items used for hexing or ill-wishing that needed to be safely destroyed could be thrown into a bonfire on this night.

It was considered lucky for those with a new home to start their fire from the coals of the festival bonfire, and anyone who started a hearth fire from the main bonfire were believed to be ensuring their own luck, fertility and wealth in the coming year (Danaher, 1972). The ashes of the fires were also viewed as having power and would be scattered in the fields to promote growth (Ó hÓgáin, 1995). In some places the harvesting tool was left out overnight in the fields (Ó Súilleabháin, 1967). This may have been for blessing purposes, to encourage a good harvest, or it may have been protective, placing iron in the fields to ward off the attentions of the Daoine Uaisle.

Other folk customs intended to improve health and banish illness included bathing on Oiche Fhéile Eoin and drinking a tea made from St. John's Wort (Ó Súilleabháin, 1967). Yarrow was hung in the house to protect against illness (Evans, 1957). It's clear looking at the different folk practices that good health was a prevalent theme among them, and many of the activities were aimed at ensuring health for a person or household, as well as the herds and crops.

In many ways this holiday ushered in the true beginning of summer, although the season had properly begun at Bealtaine. Swimming was engaged in on the holiday and it was said that those who celebrated the festival should be safe from drowning in the following year (Danaher, 1972). The holiday is also called Bonfire Night, Oiche an teine chnáimh [night of the bone fires], and Teine Féile Eoin [fire of the feast of John] (Danaher, 1972). As with most other festivals fire and water played central roles in the celebrations.

Special foods associated with this holiday include sweets and in Connacht a dish called 'goody' which was white bread soaked in warm milk laced with spices and sugar (Danaher, 1972). Drinking was also a common feature of the celebrations. The overall tone of the time was celebratory.

Midsummer was also strongly associated with both Áine and Manannán mac Lir who would be honoured at this time. Torchlit processions occurred at Cnoc Áine, with a bonfire at the summit, in honour of Áine, who was understood as one of the Tuatha Dé Danann, a queen of the Sidhe, and in some folklore a human woman taken by the Aos Sidhe. Accounts from the 20th century describe people celebrating on the hill who claim they saw Áine herself among the revellers.

Lúnasa

"To Brón Trogaill, i.e. [Lúnasa], that is., the beginning of autumn; for it is then the earth is afflicted, that is., the earth under fruit. Trogam is a name for 'earth.'" – Tochmarc Emer

Lúnasa is also called Lughnasadh, Lughnasa, or Brón Trogain. Lúnasa is the name in Irish for the month of August and the original festival is described in the Lebor Gabala Erenn as spanning a full month, beginning two weeks before the first of august and stretching two weeks afterwards. Today those who follow the calendar dates focus on the first of August, with festivities perhaps beginning the night before. Those who use astrological timing look for the sun to be at 15 degrees in Leo, around the end of the first week of August. Agrarian signs would include the beginning of the grain harvest.

The name of the festival is translated into either Middle or Old Irish as the assembly of Lugh or the funeral assembly of Lugh, with a slightly different connotation between the different periods of the language. The connection to a funeral assembly is because the celebration was originally created by the god Lugh as a memorial for his foster mother, Tailtiu, after her death, something we are told in the Lebor Gabala Erenn. The later meaning may reflect the many athletic games and competitions associated with the harvest fairs that occurred at this time. Although Tailtiu is the one most often connected to Lúnasa various local celebrations of the holiday had a different focus including Naas in the town named for her, where Lugh was said to have instituted the celebration in her memory because she was one of his wives. We might see in this a wider theme of a harvest celebration in honour of a goddess who died, perhaps as Tailtiu did clearing land for cultivation.

The other Irish name, Brón Trogain, is usually understood to mean "Earth's sorrow", with the implication of the weight of the harvest causing the earth to lament (MacNeill, 1962). Brón in older Irish as in modern Irish means sorrow; Trogain means, among other things, earth and autumn. Trogan is also associated with childbirth through the expression *"troigh mhna troghuin foruibh 'pangs of a woman in childbirth'"* (eDIL, n.d.). This metaphor for childbirth aligns well with the wider symbolism of the harvest and was likely intended as a layer of meaning in the name. This name for the holiday is mentioned in the Wooing of Emer quoted above and MacNeill suggests, based on passages from the Acallamh na Senórach, that Brón Trogain was the older name for the holiday which only later came to be known as Lúnasa.

Of the four fire festivals of the pagan Irish Lúnasa has the fewest mythical associations. It appears only once in the Lebor Gabala Erenn, as the date that the Fir Bolg invaded Ireland (MacNeill, 1962). That is perhaps an interesting crossover with the idea that the holiday itself memorialized a Fir Bolg goddess. Its celebration is mentioned in two other places: the Tochmarc Emer and the Genemain Aedh Slán. The Tochmarc Emer passage has already been quoted above and refers to the holiday as the beginning of autumn and a time of fruit. The second reference says:

> For these were the two principal gatherings that they had: Tara's Feast at every samhain (that being the heathens' Easter); and at each lughnasa, or' Lammas-tide,' the Convention of Taillte. (Jones, n.d.).

This places Lughnasa on a level of equal importance with Samhain and describes it as a time of community gathering, despite our lack of references to it more generally in myths.

In modern practice Lúnasa is celebrated at the beginning of August, however, there is evidence that the date of Lúnasa would actually have represented the starting date of a series of festivals and fairs, rather than a single one-day celebration. Harvest fairs associated with Lúnasa, called Oenacha, may last for several days, appearing from 1st August to the 12th (MacNeill, 1962). There are some hints that the dates may be hard to pin down because they were originally based on a lunar reckoning that is now lost (MacNeill, 1962). It is generally agreed though that no harvesting should be done before the correct date, represented by Lúnasa, and that to harvest before this is both bad luck and the sign of a bad farmer or poor housewife (Danaher, 1972). This folk belief persisted even into the 20th century tying Lúnasa firmly to the harvest.

At heart Lúnasa celebrates the beginning of the harvest and the new abundance of food being gathered; because of this it is strongly associated with the cooking of specific foods associated with the harvest, especially porridge and bread, often with seasonal fruit (Danaher, 1972). There is also mention of a ritualistic approach to a meal, where cows are milked in the morning and the milk used in the feast, and a special type of bread being made from harvested grain and cooked with rowan or another sacred wood before being handed out by the head of the household to the family who eats it and then walks sun-wise around the cooking fire, chanting a blessing prayer (McNeill, 1959). This period just prior to the beginning of the harvest was the leanest of the year, so that the celebration of fresh fruit, vegetables, and grains was all the more significant (MacNeill, 1962).

This may also be symbolically related to another legend of Lúnasa, the battle between the god Lugh and the mysterious mythic figure of Crom Dubh. Crom Dubh had a special day on the last Sunday of July called Domhnach Crom Dubh and possessed a dangerous bull bent on destruction that had to be stopped to preserve the harvest (Kondratiev, 1998). In modern folklore we find a range of stories in which saint Patrick battles Crom to secure the harvest, but McNeill theorizes that these stories would have originally featured the god, Lugh. Many involve saint Patrick or Lugh battling and outwitting Crom and thus ensuring the safety and bounty of the harvest; in some cases, this theme is given the additional layer of the defeat, sacrifice, consumption, and then resurrection of Crom's bull which may argue for an older element of bull sacrifice on this day (MacNeill, 1962).

Another folk practice at Lúnasa was for people, often the entire community, to gather outdoors at a traditional place; the site would be someplace beautiful and wild but remote enough that travelling to it would represent a challenge (Danaher, 1972). Other practices of Lúnasa include decorating holy wells and pillar stones, referred to as 'dressing', and also travelling to hill or mountaintops; while the celebration was widespread the particular traditions varied widely by location and could be very unique in each place, showing that holiday took on its own character regionally (MacNeill, 1962). As with most of the other fire festivals there are references to blessing cows on the eve of Lúnasa and of making charms for the cattle and milking equipment so that the blessing would remain for the year to come (McNeill, 1959). Weather focused divination was common, wherein the conditions of the day were observed and noted for the appearance and colouring of specific landmarks as well as consideration of the weather in the year so far, in order to predict what was to come (Danaher, 1972).

Lúnasa was also well known for harvest fairs and an assortment of athletic competitions and horse races; it is important to note that the ancient fairs were not intended to be occasions of commerce but were social gathering and celebration (MacNeill, 1962). Many different types of games were held, as well as competitions of agility and strength, fire leaping, and swimming races of both horses and men (Danaher, 1972). This holiday was based on the gathering of community, celebration, fresh food and the abundance of the harvest, and was a time that emphasized pleasure and joy before the real work of the harvest began.

While any pagan rituals related to Lúnasa have long since been lost there are several deities who are still associated with this holiday. The primary one Lugh, who lends his name to the holiday, who appears in stories to battles with Crom Dubh over the harvest, and is, of course, created the event to commemorate his foster mother. Tailtiu would be the next divine being connected to Lúnasa, as it commemorates her and was dedicated to her in Telltown, and we might also mention the goddess Naas who was commemorated in a similar way in Naas. In some stories the goddess Áine is associated with both a three-day period during Lúnasa and to the figure of Crom Dubh as his consort during this time (MacNeill, 1962). Another goddess who might be mentioned now is Macha, one of the three Morrignae, who some believe raced the king's horses at a Lúnasa fair; whether or not this is so there is evidence of a long-standing celebration of Lúnasa at Emain Macha and the surrounding areas in Ulster (MacNeill, 1962). The harvest itself may also be connected to the Cailleach, as it was a common custom to associate the last sheaf in the field with the her; however, this may be more appropriate later in the harvest season at Samhain (Danaher, 1972).

Pregnancy and Birth

Pregnancy was strongly emphasized in old Irish culture several of the Brehon laws addressing conception. For example, there were laws that allowed either partner to sue for divorce due to the infertility of the other partner, or in the same situation for a temporary separation of the couple in order for the fertile partner to have a child with another person (Bitel, 1996). Nonetheless I could find very little information relating to pregnancy folklore or folk practices besides those relating to conception and birth. The actual pregnancy itself is rarely discussed in sources, likely due to superstitions about bringing bad luck if it were focused on before the child was born.

What I did find was that there are a small selection of Irish superstitions relating to pregnancy. It was thought that if a pregnant woman had a hare run across her path her child would be born with a cleft lip unless she ripped the hem of her dress or skirt (Ó hÓgáin, 1995; Ó Súilleabháin, 1967). Similarly, if a pregnant woman twisted her foot in a graveyard her child would be born with a twisted foot (Ó Súilleabháin, 1967). A pregnant woman should never help prepare a corpse or attend a wake, for fear of a similar fate befalling her unborn child (Ó hÓgáin, 1995; Ó Súilleabháin, 1967). Nor should an expectant mother attend a bride, although a pregnant woman was thought to be especially lucky for a blacksmith's forge and might be asked to grant that luck to the smith by pumping the bellows (Ó Súilleabháin, 1967). Generally, it seems that the belief was that an unborn baby was easily influenced by outside circumstances and powers and so needed special protections from interference.

For issues relating to birth the goddess Brighid might be called on. In her guise as a Christian Saint she is connected to childbirth and midwifery, and the pagan holiday of Imbolc which Brighid is strongly associated with is connected to ewe's lambing (Butler, 2021).

Marriage

We do not have any fully preserved pagan wedding ceremonies, although there are many modern versions including the ever-popular handfasting. Here I would like to touch on some of what we do know about the older pagan and early conversion era marriage practices.

Early Irish law recognized nine forms of marriage in a special law text called the Cáin Lánamna, each of which conveyed a different social status, legal rights, and inheritance rights for potential children (Kelly, 2005). This ranged from a formal union that we would clearly identify as marriage today to less formal unions where the pair might not cohabitate but would visit each other at times. Who a child belonged to and who was expected to raise the child depended on the type of marriage and the feelings of each partner's kin, creating a complex web of relationships and responsibilities. As with many other pagan cultures of the time polygyny was an accepted practices and a husband was expected to pay the bride's father a bride-price for her (Kelly, 2005). Although less explicitly accepted, and only appearing in literary sources, polyandry or women taking multiple partners does appear in some stories, most notably perhaps with Queen Medb who was married to Ailill but renowned for her many lovers. In the same way while there are no known account of same sex marriages in Irish paganism there are several accounts of bisexual or homosexual relationships which didn't appear to face social backlash. One of the most prominent being a law case where a woman had sex with her husband then, shortly afterwards, with her female lover who became pregnant from the encounter; the legal question was who was responsible for the child but there is no mention of any censure or judgement about the relationship itself (Bitel, 1996).

Although modern weddings are most often in the summer pagan Irish weddings were more likely to have occurred primarily across the winter, from November through mid-February. This is because the spring, summer, and fall periods were the most active for the community, marked not only by herding and farming but also by warfare, while winter was a quieter time when people were more focused on domestic issues such as marriage (Patterson, 1994). How exactly these weddings would have been conducted is uncertain, allowing modern practitioners a lot of leeway to create what they'd like.

I should note, that divorce was a possibility in pagan Irish culture and didn't necessarily carry any stigma, although specific requirements had to be met for it such as infidelity, domestic violence, spreading negative rumours about one's spouse, or failing to provide for one's partner.

Death

As with marriage we don't have any preserved pagan funeral rites, but we do know that it was a custom to raise a cairn over a body or place a grave marker. We also have some moving literary examples of laments or poems to the dead, such as Cu Chulainn's lament after Ferdiad's death, which demonstrate one possible approach to memorializing the deceased.

Prayers

Modern Irish pagan prayers cover a wide range of possibilities, touching on every aspect of life. Historic prayers are less well attested but we do have a few examples that have survived and which most scholars feel are pagan or reflect older pagan material. I am including my own translations of these below.

Fáed Fíada – aka the Deer's Cry

The oldest part of Saint Patrick's Lorica this section is thought to date back, possibly, into the pagan period and to reference the magical ability to pass invisibly which was a skill of the Aos Sidhe and Tuatha Dé Danann.

I bind today
strength of sky
light of sun
radiance of moon
brightness of flame
swiftness of light
speed of wind
depth of ocean
steadfastness of earth
firmness of rock.

Cétnad nAíse

A poem which is also in its way a prayer and magical chant for
protection and for long life. The poem itself is difficult to parse
but Tonsing suggests in his analysis of it that it is primarily
a pagan piece with very little clear Christian influence. I am
excluding only the last four lines, which do reflect that foreign
influence.

I invoke the seven daughters of the stormy sea
shaping life's thread from boyhood to age
Three deaths be taken from me
Three ages be given to me
Seven waves of good fortune dispense to me!
No harm to me on my circuit
in flashing corslet without hindering!
Not light is my reputation before heaven!
To me these ages
May I not die until old age
I invoke my Silver warrior
who did not die and will not die
Deliver to me time
of excellent electrum!
Chanting my form,
Ennobling my authority,
Magnified my strength,
Not readied my grave,
May I not die on a journey,
My death fulfilled!
May a foolish serpent not overtake me,
Nor a hard-green worm,
Nor a senseless beetle!
May no theft destroy me
Nor host of women
Nor warrior troop!

To me extensions of time
From the King of everything!
I invoke Senach of seven-durations
Who was reared by Fairy women
on their breasts.
May my seven lights not be submerged!
I am an indestructible fort,
I am an immovable foundation,
I am that treasure
I am seven-times-valuable compensation
May I be possessing a hundred
hundred years
Every hundred from each hour.
I sue towards me my advantage

Chapter 6

Irish Magic

"Three signs of wisdom: patience, closeness, the gift of prophecy."

— *Triads of Ireland*

Entire books could and have been written about Irish magic but I would be remiss not to at least touch on the subject here, so I am going to include a selection of key aspects from the Irish which differ from other cultures and types of magic. I am, however, excluding the topics of cursing and of spoken magic, as both of those were covered thoroughly in my previous book, *Pagan Portals-Irish Paganism,* and I would rather focus on fresh ground here.

Cleansing[14]

Many aspects of how the pre-Christian Irish pagans specifically would have viewed this concept and dealt with it has been lost, of course, but hints remain and these hints as well as modern folk practices are more than enough for a person to create a viable system to work with today. When we look at the iron age Irish, we mostly find the idea of what harms people embodied as spirits (and so we see means to fight or drive off these spirits) but we do also see in some cases the idea of magic or energetic illnesses that effect people in negative ways, such as Cu Chulainn's wasting sickness or Aengus's love sickness. We also find the idea that people through their actions can place themselves into or out of society with people outside of society having a distinct and dangerous energy to them that must be purified before they return to civilization. Taking all of the evidence together can help us get an idea of the wider beliefs relating to healthy and harmful energy and how to deal with it.

We can find a few hints in mythology and ritual practices that indicate that people who intentionally stepped outside of society needed to be ritually cleansed before re-entering it. Specifically, there is indications that a person who had left society to live in a wild state and who wished to re-enter society needed to be ritually cleansed using a process that featured a ritual meal, usually a broth (McCone, 1990). This process may have involved the broth being both consumed as well as asperged over the person or symbolically bathed in. This broth would have been made from food that was being ritually offered to the gods and so was sacred by association as it were. The Fianna, who lived a portion of their time outside society, seem to have had cleansing rituals in order to re-enter society later and these rituals may have involved ritual anointing with milk or butter (PSVL, 2011). In this way we see that the food used for ritual feasting could play a role in purification, particularly the more significant or serious purifications including redeeming people who had been living wild or as outlaws.

As with many other cultures we also see the idea of burning different herbs to cleanse away baneful energy. The most well known in Irish and also Scottish culture may be juniper. Juniper is mentioned by various authors, including Danaher, Evans, and MacNeil, for its protective qualities in folk belief and for the widespread practice of burning juniper in the home and stables on the Fire Festivals to be rid of dangerous energy and to bless the space and people. Another less well-known herb burned for protection against evil spirits and baneful magic was mugwort, which was also kept around the home, tied onto livestock, and worn on a person's clothing for purification and to ward off fairies and witches (MacCoitir, 2006). Rosemary was also used especially as a fumigant in sick rooms, carrying the idea of cleansing away lingering illness or baneful energy in the atmosphere.

We don't know for certain exactly how the pre-Christian Irish viewed ideas like the Greek concept of miasma, if they even had such a concept themselves, but we do know that there were concepts relating to cleansing of a person, which allowed them to re-claim a place in society. Irish society in general was one that was very focused on reparative justice, as we see in the Brehon Laws and in the mythology (Kelly, 2005). This, perhaps, explains why the focus on purification and cleansing is the way that it is with its emphasis on returning a person to a proper alignment with society and with its focus on protecting people and their places by keeping the energy there beneficial. We also know that specific actions such as entering a space sunwise had power to bless both a space and the person and could be used for cleansing. And finally, there were practices relating to burning or wearing a variety of herbs, a few of which are mentioned here, with the belief that the smoke from these plants or their presence would cleanse away or ward off harmful energy and purify a space or person. This purification was important before engaging in any ritual activity or folk magic, and we see people engaging in such purification regularly – burning juniper on all the Quarter days, walking three times sunwise before entering a holy well, turning around three times before seeking a charm stone in a river.

For those seeking to work such magic or follow such a spirituality in a modern context maintaining a good habit of purification and cleansing is essential. Perhaps especially so for those who seek to walk a liminal way or who intentionally step outside society's bounds on a regular basis. The more baneful or harmful energy you may be around the more important it is to make sure you purify and cleanse often, but even if you live within society and keep on the straight and narrow (as it were) it's a good idea to at least purify and cleanse on the major holidays. I recommend a combination of the above-mentioned methods, although I favour incorporating moving sunwise (or depending on circumstance against the sun) into everything you do, with intention.

Visionary Practices

Now we know that there were some very specific methods used by the poets during the transition period between paganism and Christianity because two of those methods were outlawed for calling on pagan gods – which for our purposes is a good thing because it means they were written about. There were three specific practices written about and these were imbas forosna – *"manifesting knowledge"*, tenm laida *"illumination of song"*, and dichetal do chennaib *"extemporaneous poetry"*. Imbas forosnai involves preparing and eating meat (referenced as pig, cat, or dog specifically), making an offering to the gods with specific chants and then lying down with the hands covering the eyes and sleeping or meditating for up to three days undisturbed to receive knowledge or an answer. Another version of this may be the tarbh feis which involves the sacrifice of a bull, eating its flesh and then wrapping up in its hide for the same purpose. The practice of retreating into a dark room, wrapped in a cloak to receive inspiration – possibly a later version of imbas forosnai – was seen in the Scottish Highlands until a few hundred years ago as found in *Description of the Western Isles of Scotland*, 1695. Tenm laida seems to be, based on its appearance in myths, a type of light trance that a person could enter to answer specific questions, sometimes associated with touching the object directly and others with putting the tips of your fingers or thumb in your mouth, such as in the stories of Finn mac Cool. In some stories it appears as a method to read the past or identify a body, although this also appears to be a type of Seership practiced by both Scathach and Fidelm in mythology when answering questions about the future. Both of these methods were outlawed by the Christian Church for calling on "idols"; the third method is dichetal do chenaib which seems to resemble tenm laida but involves a deeper trance and the spontaneous speaking of poetry to answer the question. Perhaps the Prophecy of the Morrigan could be viewed as this type of method. Dichetal do chenaib was not outlawed as it didn't directly call on pagan deities or spirits and was seen as a part of the poet's art.

Additionally, we have references in myths and other stories to the pagan Irish using particular types of divination such as casting lots and a variety of omens including ornithomancy, or divination by observing the flight of birds. In the story of Donn, we learn that he was chosen to sacrifice himself to defeat the Tuatha Dé Danann's magic through choosing lots, and in the Cét-Cath Maige Tuired the arrival of the Tuatha Dé is foretold to the Fir Bolg king through a dream of a flock of black birds. Two poems survived in a text called Fiachairecht & Dreanacht or Raven Augury and Wren Augury, which explains how to interpret omens through ravens or wrens respectively. There is an excellent book called *Birds of Ireland Facts, Folklore, and History* by Anderson that has a lot of the older folklore about each type of bird including older folk beliefs about omens associated with them.

Ogham

The Ogham Tract is one of the most interesting and useful texts to study for those interested in Irish mythology and divination. Within the text the mythological origins of Ogham are outlined and several different types of Ogham are discussed, although only the Tree Ogham and Word Oghams are gone into with any depth. The sections detailing these two types of Ogham are invaluable, however, for those who seek to use the Ogham for divination since they attach significant meaning to each letter, and these meanings can be used as the basis for a system of symbolism.

The first section looks at the mythological history of the Ogham, using the typical question and answer style so often seen in Irish texts. The first question asks about the place, time, inventor and cause of the creation of the Ogham and the answer, while apocryphal, are illuminating. We learn that the Ogham was created in Ireland during the time that Bres ruled the Tuatha Dé Danann, before mortals came to Ireland, and that it was invented by the god Ogma to prove his inventiveness and to give the educated something the uneducated didn't have. This tells us not only that the Ogham is believed to have divine origins, but also that it is believed to have been created as something to be reserved for a select few. The second questions asked relate to why it is called Ogham, who are the "father" and "mother" of the Ogham, what was first written in it and why "b" is the primary letter. The name is explained as a play on words from og-uaim meaning perfect alliteration and is an allusion to the poets' art and possibly the very mnemonics that are used to remember the meanings of each letter in each type of Ogham. The father of Ogham is, of course, Ogma, and the mother is said to be his hand or blade; this is a beautiful description of the balanced act of creation involving both passive design and active carving. The final answer contains another fascinating bit of mythology, that is that the first thing written was "b" and that it was written as a warning to the god Lugh that his wife was about to be kidnapped to Faery. Interestingly it is said that "b", which in tree Ogham is associated with birch, was written seven times on a switch of birch; this not only reinforces the connection between the letter and the tree but also offers a possible magic charm to be used.

After this section the divisions of Ogham are discussed, with the idea of dividing the Ogham into four groups of five. It also mentioned that they can be separated into three groups of eight based on the Tree Ogham, divided by chieftain trees, peasant trees, and shrub trees. A second origin of Ogham is mentioned, the school of Fenius, which adds three diphthongs to the twenty consonants and vowels. Then a brief outline of the Tree Ogham is given, followed by the more in-depth description of the Tree and Word Oghams, and then very brief descriptions of many other types of Ogham.

By studying the trees associated with each letter and then the descriptions given for each correspondence to the Word Ogham a clear pattern of symbols can be developed for use in divination. Using the Ogham for divination can be effective and useful if the symbolism of each letter is fully understood. Many people err in only looking to the Tree Ogham for meaning when divining with the letters, when in fact the other types of Ogham reinforce and add detail and depth of meaning providing clearer readings. Ogham can easily be used as the primary means of divination for both personal daily use and at ritual, but it is important to understand the meanings of each letter as fully as possible. Interestingly the "Boy Ogham" is actually a method of divination in and of itself that uses the mother's name written in Ogham to predict the gender of her unborn child by dividing the name at a certain point, which is unfortunately not specified in the text.

The Ogham Tract may at first seem of interest only to those seeking to learn about divination since that is what Ogham is most known for these days, yet the tract contains valuable mythology as well. Studying this text is useful to anyone because it expands our knowledge of Irish mythology with small details and also highlights the exclusive place of Ogham literacy when the Tract was written. And of course, it is invaluable for those seeking to use the Ogham for divination as well. No matter what your focus is, if you are interested in studying the Ogham, this text is useful and should be studied.

Over the years I have come up with what I call my "Ogham Quick Reference Guide" to help me out when I'm using ogham for ritual omens or divination. Due to a learning disability, I've found the ogham especially challenging to learn and using this little guide has been helpful, so I have previously shared it publicly and am including it here, but these should be understood as my own ideas based on the source material.

English letter: B
Ogham name: Beithe – pronounced: Beh
Literally "birch tree": new beginnings, cleansing, protection.

English letter: L
Ogham name: Luis – pronounced Looh-sh
Possibly from the Old Irish "lus", herb. In tree ogham represents the Rowan, "coarthann": Enchantment, mysticism, protection against magic.

TTT

English letter: F
Ogham name: Fearn – Pronounced Fee-yarn
The alder tree, Old Irish "fern", modern "fearnog": support, protection during attack. Often associated with ravens and divination.

English letter: S
Ogham name: Saille – Pronounced Sall-yuh
The willow tree, Old Irish "sail": healing, making plans,
moving forward.

English letter: N
Ogham name: Nuin – pronounced Noo-in
Possibly "weaver's beam". In the tree ogham associated with
the Ash, "fuinseag": peace, creation, stability. A clear path.
Bring things together.

English letter: H
Ogham name: Huath – pronounced Oo-uh
Literally terror or phantom. In the tree Ogham represented by
the Hawthorn, "sceach" a fairy tree: the unknown, fear of the
unseen, transition.

English letter: D
Ogham name: Duir – pronounced Doo-ihr
The oak "dair": wisdom, strength, protection, growth.

English letter: T
Ogham name: Tinne – pronounced Tihn-nyeh
Literally means metal rod. In the tree ogham associated with the Holly "cuileann": fighting, contention, weapons, fire, and smithcraft.

English letter: C
Ogham name: Coll – pronounced Kohl
Means hazel: divination, magic, and enchantment, knowledge. Also relates to wealth.

English letter: Q
Ogham name Quert, alt. Cert – pronounced Kehrt
Means "rags". In the tree ogham this is apple "ull": healing, restoration, renewal, nourishment.

English letter: M
Ogham name: Muin – pronounced Mwin

Literally means "neck" or "back". In the tree ogham it stands for the vine "funiuin": release, compromises, focus, determination, confrontation, vengeance (basically think the good and bad sides of wine).

English letter: G
Ogham name: Gort – pronounced Guhrt
Literally "field". In the tree ogham it is the ivy, "eidhnean": beauty, love, friendship, fidelity.

English letter: nG
Ogham name nGetal – pronounced Neh-tahl
Literally "wounding". Associated with the broom plant or reed "giolcach" in tree ogham: separation, warning, courage, direct action.

English letter: Str
Ogham name: Straif – pronounced Strahf
Literally "sulfur". In the tree ogham it is the blackthorn "draighean": discernment, cunning, focused protection, the thorn, inner strength, boundaries.

English letter: R
Ogham name: Ruis – pronounced Roosh
Literally "redness". In tree ogham it represents the elder tree,
"trom": anger, blushing (i.e. loss of face, embarrassment),
endings, completion, be realistic in order to succeed.

English letter; A
Ogham name; Ailm – pronounced Al-ihm
The word and its meaning are uncertain. In tree ogham it
represents the fir or pine, "giuis": hard work, effort. The need
for caution. Integrity and good judgment are key.

English letter: O
Ogham name: Onn – pronounced On
Old Irish for "ash tree" or "stone". In tree ogham this is
given as gorse, "aitenn": take action, movement, success,
perseverance, relief.

English letter: U
Ogham name: Uir – pronounced Oor

Literally "earth". Associated in tree ogham with heather, "fraoch": embrace your talents, plant now to harvest later, effort brings reward with patience.

English letter: E
Ogham name: Edad – pronounced Ehd-ahd
The word and meaning are unknown. In the tree ogham it is the aspen, "crithach": endings, death, let go of what you've outgrown. Calm consideration. Trust in your ability to endure.

English letter: I
Ogham name: Idad – pronounced Eed-ahd
The word and meaning are unknown. Associated with the yew, "iur", in the tree ogham: see the big picture. Seek experience, know when to act and when not act. Bide your time. Don't avoid problems.

Further reading on the Ogham:

Ogam: Weaving Words of Wisdom by Erynn Rowan Laurie
Ogam: the Celtic Oracle of the Trees by Paul Rhys Montfort
Ogham, the Secret Language of the Druids by Robert Ellison
The Poet's Ogham by John-Paul Patton

Geasa
We see personal prohibitions or directives in many different religions including mainstream monotheistic ones, particularly

around food where a religion might declare a certain food off limits for followers of that religion, or in turn might require the consumption of something. In historic Irish paganism these prohibitions and directives would be called geasa (singular geis), although it should be understood that geasa were not taken lightly. Except where they are specific to a role, like kingship, they were for life and once in place remained in place until the person died.

A geis is something the you either must do or must not do in order to maintain your luck and health, and breaking a geis means certain doom usually orchestrated by Otherworldly powers. We can find a wide array of examples of geasa in Irish mythology from those placed on kings when they took the crown to those of a more personal nature that might be given at birth. A prohibitive example might be taken from Da Derga's Hostel were Conaire isn't supposed to invite a person alone into a place he staying in after sunset, while in contrast a directive geis would be seen with Fergus's requirement always to accept hospitality offered to him. Geasa are never, in stories, taken on by a person but are always placed on a person by an outside force or power. They also in many examples relate to an individual's spiritual connection to an animal, other being, or group; we see this in Conaire's geis not to hunt birds to whom he was related through his Otherworldly father, Cu Chulainn's not to eat dog meat since he was connected to that animal through his name, and Diarmuid's not to hunt the Otherworldly boar that his fate was bound to.

Some people argue that geasa only apply to kings, heroes, and other very rare important people based on the examples we have from mythology but I think there is a strong argument from folklore that the idea behind geasa was applied to many people across demographics in different ways. Although I might not call them geasa in the modern world the underlying concept of something that must be done or not done to maintain one's luck and health remains true. Yeats relaying an anecdote about a fairy doctor relates specific habits and dietary restrictions, such as not drinking alcohol or eating meat, which were strictly adhered to and had clear spiritual overtones. Cultural or communal prohibitions, such as not disturbing fairy mounds, also argue for a wider application of this concept.

In modern spirituality a person might acquire such a sacred prohibition when they achieve some type of initiation; for example, when I became a priestess of the Othercrowd I was given a prohibition not to cut my hair. Interestingly I know several people who have a similar prohibition against hair-cutting for different spiritual reasons in paganism. Such a thing could come from the person initiating you, from the gods in whatever form you feel such messages come, or may be a standard thing in your tradition for that type of ceremony. Becoming a priest or priestess in particular often seems to come with a sacred prohibition or prohibitions for people. As with the older concept, these prohibitions are generally permanent and cannot be transgressed without serious consequences for the person, and so should not be taken lightly or viewed as something to jump into getting.

A sacred prohibition can also come in the modern world through pure personal gnosis, although I will personally caution here that in these cases because of the gravity of these prohibitions I always recommend double or triple checking the message. This can be done by asking a neutral third party – someone who has no stake in the answer – who is good at divination or channelling to see if they get the same or a similar message. To use myself as an example again (because I don't like using other people as examples without permission) I also have a prohibition from Themselves not to enter into a Christian church or any place where active Christian worship is being conducted; as I have no dispute with Christianity myself this prohibition surprised me and I was careful to get it verified before accepting it as genuine. People may have prohibitions through personal gnosis that could include an array of different things but the most common ones I have seen or heard of relate to food, drink, hair, or the need to always do or say something specific at certain time or place.

Sacred prohibitions in the modern world are not a subject we discuss often, nor are they an aspect of modern spirituality that is often focused on. Yet the core idea of having a spiritual prohibition or directive is not uncommon in my experience and is something that I not only have myself but also that I know many other people who have. These prohibitions or directives can impact a person's life in ways that may include social aspects, and I think for that fact alone it's worth wider understanding and consideration.

Wands and Sacred Woods[15]

When we look at Irish mythology, we see many instances of Druids using wands, as well as those who are not explicitly Druids but who are acquainted with Druidic magic, such as Fionn mac Cumhail. The story of Fionn includes the use of wands, generally made of hazel; it is a hazel wand that turns Fionn's wife into a deer, and in some translations, it is a hazel wand that prospective members of the Fianna must use to defend themselves with when undergoing trials before being accepted, and one version of a story about Fionn has him using a hazel wand for divination (although most versions have him biting on his thumb). In some versions of the story of the Children of Lir as well a wand is used to curse the four children into the shape of swans and in the Wooing of Etain the druid Dalan uses three wands made of yew to divine the location of Etain.

Oak was known and mentioned as sacred in Ireland, but it is the hazel and rowan that were most well-known and associated with the magic (McNeill, 1959). It is believed that the ancient Irish revered hazel, rowan, elder, and hawthorn in particular, with yew and ash also mentioned in some sources (Evans, 1957; Wilde, 1991). Even into the last century hazel and rowan were viewed as protective and blessing in Irish folklore (Ó Súilleabháin, 1967).

The rowan was seen as a lucky wood and was considered to be the best protection against negative magic; it is also considered by some to provide the berries that are the food of the Aos Sidhe (McNeill, 1959). Rowans were often planted by the front door of the home to protect it and rowan wood was used to make sacred fires to cook the little cakes often featured in folk ceremonies (McNeill, 1959). Some also believe that rowan was the wood used by the Irish Druids to create sacred fires for their rituals (Estyn Evans, 1957). In modern practice the rowan is sometimes associated with the goddess Brighid. On Bealtaine sprigs of Rowan were hung above cradles, churns, and doorways to protect them from fairy influence (Wilde, 1991).

The hazel was both seen as useful in magic, as a wand, and also connected to wisdom as hazelnuts were believed to provide knowledge. We see this in the story of Fionn, who eats a salmon that has eaten the hazelnuts of the well of Segais and gains the wisdom of the world. It was believed that a hazel wand cut on Bealtaine had the greatest power, and that a person could use such a wand to trace a circle in the ground around themselves which would be a sure protection against fairies and evil spirits (Wilde, 1991). Besides protection, particularly from faeries, hazel was also associated with healing especially of poison (Danaher, 1964). As we've noted hazel wands appear in mythology used by Druids to transform and to divine.

The elder seems to have a contradictory nature, being used for healing and making musical instruments like flutes, but also used in cursing; it is said that striking a living thing with an elder twig will cause illness or death (Danaher, 1964).

The apple has a long history in Irish lore, being associated with magic, healing, and long life. In myth, the apple branch is used to gain entry to the Otherworld, and is strongly associated with the Aos Sidhe. As Evans Wentz says in the epic *Fairy Faith in Celtic Countries:*

> *For us there are no episodes more important than those in the ancient epics concerning these apple-tree talismans, because in them we find a certain key which unlocks the secret of that world from which such talismans are brought, and proves it to be the same sort of a place as the Otherworld of the Greeks and Romans. (Evans Wentz, 1911).*

Many modern Druids use an apple branch decked with bells to open the way to the Otherworld during ritual, and to invite in good spirits.

Both the blackthorn and hawthorn were dual natured, seen as both protective and also as fairy trees that could be dangerous (Ó Súilleabháin, 1967). The hawthorn has many associations with Bealtaine. It may have been significant in part because of its flowers and berries, with the white flowers representing the hope of spring and its red berries the fulfillment of the harvest (Estyn Evans, 1957). While Hawthorns planted by people, or found in hedges, were not seen as special the lone Hawthorn was said to be a fairy tree and not to be disturbed or damaged (Estyn Evans, 1957). Hawthorn is considered one of the seven herbs of great power by Lady Wilde, along with elder tree bark, ivy, vervain, eyebright, groundsel, and foxglove (Wilde, 1991).

Finally, the yew also plays a role in the Irish approach to magical trees. As mentioned, we see a Druid using yew wands in the Wooing of Etain for the purpose of divination. The yew was renowned for its long life and was one of the trees about which it was thought that trimming would bring bad luck (Danaher, 1964). In modern folklore the yew is associated with death, but this is not likely to have been how the ancients saw it as the modern view is largely based on the fact that yews are often found in growing in church graveyards.

Anyone looking to incorporate the use of trees, wood, or wands into the practice of Irish polytheism would do well, at the least, to focus on hazel and rowan. Including the other trees mentioned here – elder, apple, blackthorn, hawthorn, and yew – would also be useful. Studying the tree ogham for each of the mentioned trees is also helpful at adding depth to their symbolism and uses.

Chapter 7

Taking It Home

"Three speeches that are better than silence: inciting a king to battle, spreading knowledge, praise after reward."

— *Triads of Ireland*

Everything that has been discussed so far represents the core of Irish pagan belief and practice, but this section will wrap up with a look at various ways that these things can be actively incorporated into a person's life, should they choose to do so. This will include a particular emphasis on ethics, as they tend to form the basis of everything else in ancient Irish paganism and should be strongly considered in modern practice as well. We will also briefly touch on the value of the Irish language, which is probably at least somewhat self-evident but still worth mentioning.

Ethics

As with everything else there are no firmly agreed on set of ethics within historic or modern Irish paganism, so what follows will largely be my own opinion, shored up with references from myth or older texts. I've drawn particularly from the Audacht Morainn and the Tecosca Cormaic here as they include some pertinent advice on how to live one's life in right relation with the world. None of this necessarily reflects the reality of lived ethics in pagan Ireland but rather the ideal that was described in literature and which was embedded in the culture.

Hospitality – Hospitality was seen as an obligation in the ancient world across all cultures, as it was essential for survival. People who were travelling were expected to be given certain things by those they encountered, for example, and being able to host others well was a sign of status. In pre-Modern Ireland there were expectations on different strata of society, particularly nobility, to provide feasts on special occasions for those who served them, just as the non-nobility were expected to provide supplies and animals to the nobility (Patterson, 1994). Society was largely reciprocal and so there were expectations of hospitality and of guest behaviour that reinforced each other. Being welcoming and being a good host and guest are still important things today.

Honour or Right Action – The concept of personal honour as well as familial honour was key in older Irish society as relayed through the myths and tales. People who are honourable do the right thing, while people who are dishonourable do not and their reputation suffers for it. There was a concept found in older Irish sources called fír fer, literally men's truth, which is often understood as fair play; it was not honourable to fight against an opponent who wasn't equally armed and matched. Because of this you will see accounts in takes where combat between two people is delayed until one can properly outfit themselves for the fight. It would have been understood by an audience when characters attacked without this fír fer that they were being dishonourable and underhanded. In the Cét-Cath Maige Tuired, when Nuada loses his arm against the Fir Bolg champion Sreng, he offers to resume the fight if Sreng will tie one of his hands behind his back to make the combat fair; Sreng refuses. When Cu Chulainn insults the Morrigan in the Táin Bó Regamna she promises to attack him during the Táin Bó Cúailgne when he is in equal combat with a matched opponent, to effectively destroy fair combat so that he loses, as a repayment for his offense to her. When Macha is forced to race the king's horses and gives birth to her twins after winning one of them is named Fial meaning 'Honourable'. These examples of unfairness illustrate the contrasting concept of fairness that underpinned the culture, at least in the ideal.

Truth – Truth is a major quality emphasized in many stories and mentioned in several of the Irish Triads. When Macha races the king's horses and births her twins, one of them is named Fír meaning 'true' or 'truth'. In the Accalamh Senórach when saint Patrick asks the last member of the Fianna what maintained the warriors in their lives, Caoilte responds "Truth in our hearts, strength in our arms, and fulfilment in our hearts". There are an assortment of special terms in older Irish relating to this concept including 'fír catha', true battle meaning a just cause, 'fír flatha' or ruler's truth, and 'fír ngascid' meaning fairness in a fight (eDIL, 2024). There is also a deep cultural understanding that speaking un-truths could have immediate consequences, especially for those in power – a poet who speaks an untrue satire against a person will have a blemish appear on their face, as will a judge who speaks a false judgment.

Moderation – the key lessons in both the Audacht Morainn and the Tecosca Cormaic relate to moderation. Life is seen as best lived if extremes are avoided and a happy medium is found. There's no better way to summarize than to quote the Tecosca Cormaic here:

"Be not too wise, be not too foolish
be not too conceited, nor too diffident
be not too haughty, nor too humble
be not too talkative, nor too silent
be not too hard, nor too soft
If you be too wise, one will expect too much of you
If you be foolish, you will be deceived
If you be too conceited, you will be thought vexatious

If you be too humble, you will be without honour
If you be too talkative, you will not be heeded
If you be too silent, you will not be regarded
If you be too hard, you will be broken
If you be too soft, you will be crushed"
(Meyer, n.d.)

Causing Harm

It is very widely known in many forms of neopaganism that any kind of harm is frowned on or considered unethical. Let's look at some of what we know of historic Irish pagan morality relating to causing harm to get an idea of how this is different here.

There are several examples in Irish lore that support the idea that violence was seen as being a necessity at times. From the triads of Ireland:

Three deaths that are better than life: the death of a salmon, the death of a fat pig, the death of a robber" and: *"Three bloodsheds that need not be impugned: the bloodshed of battle, of jealousy, of mediating.*

Although the Brehon laws emphasize compensation over corporal punishment, the death penalty was a reality in Ireland. In the case of a homicide, for example, if the person refused to go before a Brehon or if he could not or would not pay the levied fine then he could lawfully be killed (Joyce, 1908). No Brehon would ever order physical punishments, as paying a fine was the standard legal punishment for any crime, but nonetheless punishments including death and blinding were common (Joyce, 1908). What this tells us is that while violence in criminal cases wasn't advocated, it was socially acceptable for such punishments to occur.

Irish pagan ethics appear to be based on the idea of personal responsibility and accepting the consequences of any action.

There was an understanding of harm as having a place within the greater workings and balance of the world, and people are expected to accept the consequences of their own actions, even if that consequence is harmful to them. The natural world is expected to endure some harm in support of human life. Even nature itself includes a balance between harm and life that is normative; natural forest fires destroy yet also clear the way for new growth, and life is often predicated on some level of harm to other living things.

I believe that the ultimate lessons of such ethics are Truth and moderation, as discussed above, even when applied to a topic like harm and violence. Truth is an understanding of the nature of reality and of living in correct alignment with that reality; when I manifest Truth in my life then I also manifest positive qualities in the world around me. Another aspect of this is good judgment, since a person who is embracing Truth should consequently be able to correctly understand the nature of other things and reach correct judgments about them. Moderation is another key aspect, where a person should be generous without being careless, ambitious without being over-reaching, and brave without being foolish, for example. If these other ethics are applied then violence or harm should only exist within a framework of need, and with an understanding of consequences for actions.

What to Avoid

The main actions or traits that are condemned seem to be greed and lust. From the Triads of Ireland: *"The three chief sins: avarice, gluttony, lust"*. A variety of the Brehon laws look at legislating states of marriage, sexual relations, and theft (I suggest reading Fergus Kelly's *A Guide to Early Irish Law* for more on this). In some of the existing prophecies relating to the future or end of the world, such as the one given by Ferchetne in the Colloquy of Two Sages or the Morrigan's prophecy in the Cath Maige Tuired, a lot of emphasis is placed on the lack of honor, lack of modesty, false judgments, lack of truth, and a general going against the natural order of things that will occur. Similarly, the Audacht Morainn and the Tescosa Cormaic emphasize the importance of the king manifesting Truth, good judgment, generosity, and moderate behaviour in order to uphold the bounty and prosperity of the land; this included being ambitious, invading neighbours, and punishing criminals. In this approach there was clearly a link between correct ethics and behaviour and the success or failure of life and the world itself, but those ethics, in general, seem to be directed at preserving the correct order of the world rather than improving it or idealizing it. People are not urged to abstain from alcohol or sex, or even violence, but to engage in those things in moderation and within the socially correct context; only when the actions exceed social acceptance or defy social order are there consequences.

Learning Irish

Speaking the Irish language is not required to practice Irish paganism, but it is often encouraged. Although you will often hear people claiming Irish is a very difficult language to learn that is usually because people find the pronunciation hard, as it uses a Latin alphabet but different associated sounds. This can prove tricky at first although once you understand that the letters represent different sounds than English it may be easier. Because Irish is a fairly popular language there are a lot of resources available to learn, everything from classes to books to online courses through programs like Rosetta Stone or FutureLearn. The internet also offers a plethora of resources for pronunciation, and platforms like TikTok and Youtube have videos by native speakers and teachers which share information.

At the very least I do encourage people to learn enough of the basics to correctly pronounce deity names and terms. I have chosen to use the Irish names and terms in this book in part because I think it's important for those interested in Irish paganism to connect to this material with as little of the colonial overlay as possible, as much as possible. The Irish language is important to understanding and connecting to the culture, and the culture is a key aspect of everything. Tir gan teanga, tir gan anam, as the saying goes.

Another good reason to learn at least the basics of the language is that there is a lot – and I mean a lot – of bad info that goes around about Irish words, terms, and names in pagan books, coming from people who don't speak or read the language. Never trust a person who doesn't speak a language or at least have a basic knowledge of it to interpret words or terms in that language. Always double or triple check with reliable sources, preferably native speakers (for modern Irish). I strongly encourage people as well not to rely on cosmological or esoteric extrapolations of Irish words coming from people without a background in the language. Irish is a living language with modern speakers and the words do in fact have meanings that exist and can't just be redefined by those outside. And even older Irish terms exist within a very specific context. It isn't a free for all, just make it up as you go, situation.

If you choose to learn Irish it should be kept in mind that old and middle Irish are separate languages distinct from modern Irish – you won't be able to read the older myths if you learn modern Irish. But you will be able to access a lot of new stories, folklore, and retellings which are invaluable.

Online dictionary resources for modern Irish:

https://www.teanglann.ie/en/fuaim/
https://www.focloir.ie/

Part II

Chapter 8

The Tuatha Dé Danann

"Three wonders of Connaught:
The grave of Eothaile on its strand. It is as high as the
strand. When the sea rises, it is as high as the tide.
The stone of the Dagda. Though it be thrown into the
sea, though it be put into a house under lock, it emerges
out of the well at which it is.
The two herons in Scattery Island. They let no other
herons to them into the island, and the she-heron goes
on the ocean westwards to hatch and returns thence
with her young ones. And coracles have not discovered
the place of hatching."

— Triads of Ireland

The Tuatha Dé Danann comprise a diverse group of beings all belonging to the same tribe, who represent the bulk of deities that are considered the gods and goddesses of Ireland. As with everything else there is some debate about the origin of these beings, whether they represent indigenous Irish deities or later literary characters, however, they are referred to as gods even in the material written by Christian scribes and have been regarded and worshipped as such for a long time, so we will treat them that way here without engaging in the debate.

The name Tuatha Dé Danann is actually of uncertain meaning although it is most often translated as 'people of the Goddess Danu'; other options are possible and John Carey suggests 'People of the Gods of Skill' (Carey, 1981). It is also worth noting that the oldest form of the term seems to have been simply Tuatha Dé, People of the gods, with Danann added on later to distinguish from the Biblical use of Tuatha Dé to mean people of God, i.e. the Israelites.

The Tuatha Dé Danann were the fifth group of beings to invade and settle in Ireland, themselves descended from the Nemedians who were the third group to settle Ireland. When they arrived, they encountered the Fir Bolg, also descendants of Nemed, who had taken over Ireland previously, and were forced to fight for a place. In this battle, told in the Cét-Cath Maige Tuired, the Tuatha Dé Danann king, Nuada, lost his arm fighting a champion of the Fir Bolg; to settle the fight at that point the Fir Bolg were offered Connacht, while the Tuatha Dé took control of the other provinces.

It was very popular for scholars across the last several centuries to apply a Classical lens to Irish myth and attempt to fit all Irish belief into that box, no matter how poorly it fits. This has resulted in an approach to the Irish gods as 'gods of' specific things in the way that Greek or Roman gods would be understood, even though that structure doesn't work well with Irish belief. Rather than a 'god of the sun' or 'god of harvest' we find that Irish belief tended to be very regional with local deities handling an array of things for the people who worshipped them. That isn't to say that the Irish gods didn't have purviews associated with them, but rather that they weren't limited to narrow concepts but had a more all-encompassing approach.

The section that follows is meant to be an overview of various named deities, rather than a deep dive into their lore. Each entry will offer some of the key facts and information about the deity beings discussed. Due to the nature of the source material, there are some beings that we have a great deal of information about and others that may only appear in a handful of references, so the amount of text for each one will inevitably vary considerably. This does to some degree reflect which deities were more popular but also which ones best survived the conversion to Christianity. It's also worth keeping in mind that the named beings we are aware of are by no means the entirety of the Tuatha Dé Danann who are clearly described as a nation of people, and even in later folklore, as the Aos Sidhe, were said to be as numerous as blades of grass. Now, let's explore some of the ones we do know about.

Áine

Like most Irish deities Áine has a complex and sometimes contradictory mythology. She is said in some sources to be the daughter of Manannán Mac Lir and in others to be the daughter of Manannán's foster son Eogabail, a Druid of the Tuatha Dé Danann (Ellis, 1987). No mother is listed for her. Some sources say that her sister is Finnen, whose name means white (Monaghan, 2004). Her name likely means "brightness" or "splendour" and she is often associated with the sun Ó hÓgáin, 2006; Monaghan, 2004). In fact, not far from her hill of Cnoc Áine is another hill, Cnoc Gréine, associated with the goddess Grian (literally "Sun") who is also reputed be a Fairy Queen; MacKillop suggests the two goddesses might represent the summer and winter suns respectively and some sources list them as sisters (MacKillop, 1998; Monaghan, 2004).

There is some confusion in modern mythology where Áine is seen as an aspect of Anu or the Morrigan, but Berresford Ellis sees this connection as unlikely (Berresford Ellis, 1987). Interestingly, Grian is similarly seen as a possible aspect of Macha, probably due to a reference to Macha in the Metrical Dindshenchas that gives an epithet of Grian to her. While I disagree with these associations, I admit that I find it fascinating that Áine and Grian are strongly associated with each other and a possible division of the year, and each is also associated with the Morrigan and Macha respectively. There is also a trend at describing Áine as a moon goddess, although there is nothing in myth or folklore to support that.

In much of her later folklore, Áine is reputed to have love affairs with mortals and several Irish families claim descent from her. The most well-known of these human descendants is the third Earl of Desmond, Gearoid Iarla. It is said by some that Gearoid did not die but was taken into Loch Guirr and would return one day (Berresford Ellis, 1987). Other tales say that he lives still within the lake and can be seen riding beneath the water on a white fairy horse, while still other stories claim that Áine turned him into a goose on the shore of the lake (Berresford Ellis, 1987). She was also said to have been raped by King Aillil Olom, on Samhain, who stories say she either bit an ear off of or she killed in punishment (Monaghan, 2004; Berresford Ellis, 1987; Ó hÓgáin, 2006). The child of this union was Eogan, whose line went on to claim rulership of the land through their descent from the goddess (Monaghan, 2004).

Áine is associated with fertility, agriculture, sovereignty, and the sun, as well as love (Berresford Ellis, 1987; Monaghan, 2004). She is associated especially with red mares, with some people claiming she could assume this form (MacKillop, 1998; Monaghan, 2004). She may also be associated more generally with horses, and possibly with geese and sheep as they appear in her folklore. The hill of Cnoc Áine is one of the most well-known places associated with her, said to have been named after her during the settling of Ireland when she used magic to help her father win the area (Ó hÓgáin, 2006). Midsummer was her special holy day and up until the 19th century people continued to celebrate her on the eve of Midsummer with a procession around the hill, carrying torches of burning straw in honor of Áine na gClair, Áine of the Wisps (Berresford Ellis, 1987). Áine is also sometimes called Áine Chlair, a word that may relate to wisps or may be an old name for the Kerry or Limerick area (Monaghan, 2004; Ó hÓgáin, 2006). On midsummer, clumps of straw would be lit on her hill and then scattered through the cultivated fields and cows to propitiate Áine's blessing (Ó hÓgáin, 2006). In county Louth there is a place called Dun Áine where people believe that the weekend after Lughnasa belongs to Áine, and in some folklore she is said to be the consort of Crom Cruach during the three days of Lughnasa (Ó hÓgáin, 2006; MacNeill, 1962). Additionally, there is another hill called Cnoc Áine in county Derry, and a third in Donegal (Ó hÓgáin, 2006). In Ulster there is a well called Tobar Áine that bears her name.

Whether a goddess or Fairy Queen, Áine, has been much loved, even up until fairly recently. Her mythology is convoluted but fascinating and any who feel the need or desire to honor a solar goddess within an Irish framework would do well to learn more about Áine. I have honored her on midsummer for many years, and am glad I do. As they say, she is "the best hearted woman who ever lived" (Ó hÓgáin, 2006).

Airmed

Also spelled Airmid, Airmeith and Airmedh, she is the daughter of the healing god, Dian Cécht and sister of Miach, Ormiach, Ochtriuil, Cu, Cethan, Cian, and Etan. The main myth in which she appears tells of the healing of King Nuada's arm by her brother, Miach; this angered Dian Cécht who killed him and when Airmed spread her cloak over his grave she found healing herbs growing from the site and harvested them; she laid all the herbs out on her cloak and organized them to preserve the knowledge of their properties. Some sources say the herbs numbered 365, with one for each of his sinews and joints, and one for every possible bodily ailment. Her father came and scattered all of the herbs, but nonetheless she is strongly associated today with herbal healing. In a later incident in the Cath Maige Tuired she appears with her father and brothers Miach (now alive again) and Ormiach to work at the healing well of Slaine, helping to heal and revive the Tuatha Dé warriors wounded in battle. Her name is probably related to a word for a measure of grain.

Anu

Anu is an obscure figure, and somewhat controversial because of the lack of solid sources about her. Her name in older Irish appears as Anand or Anann, probably meaning abundance. There are two hills in County Kerry named for her, the Dá Chich Anann [two breasts of Anu]. In the one recension of the Lebor Gabala Erenn we are told that Anu is the proper name of the Morrigan, although that is contradicted in other versions. In the same way some people feel that Anu and Danu are identical beings, and that Danu is a confusion of Dea Anu, goddess Anu, although this is only supposition.

Badb

Badb is an Irish war goddess, particularly well known in the north west; Boa island in County Fermanagh, Northern Ireland, is named for her. Badb, also spelled Badhbh or Bodb, means a hooded crow, deadly, dangerous, warlike, and venomous (eDIL, 2024). The hooded crow is a form taken by Badb as well as the Morrigan, although it's unclear whether the term came to be associated with hooded crows because of the goddess or the other way around. The word is also used to describe different types of supernatural women, sometimes translated as witch in English. She may also be called Badb Catha, or battle crow, causing some people to relate her to the Gaulish Cathbodua.

In mythology Badb is described as both a sister of the Morrigan and given the title of Morrigan herself, and in the same way her name is also used as a title both for other deities and for human witches, causing some confusion in texts. She is a daughter of Ernmas, along with her sisters Macha and the Morrigan, as well as another triad of sisters, Eriu, Fotla, and Banba, and is said to have two children, Ferr Doman and Fiamain (Macalister, 1941; Gray, 1983). According to the Banshenchus she is the wife of the Dagda, and she is also sometimes said to be the wife of the war god Neit, an obscure figure that we have almost no information about.

In some versions of the Tain Bo Cúailgne, Badb appears inciting Cu Chulain to fight, and in the story of Cu Chulainn's death she appears in the form of a crow and flies over him signalling to his enemies that he has died (Smyth, 1988; Green, 1992). She is able to influence battle because her cries cause confusion, panic, and chaos among warriors; it is said that in the 9th century she appeared during a battle and incited a slaughter (Green, 1992; Ó hÓgáin, 2006). In the Cét-Cath Maige Tuired the Fir Bolg poet, upon seeing the carnage of the battle, declares that "The Red Badb will thank them for the battle-combats I look on".

Besides slaughter and war, Badb is often linked to prophecy. After the battle of Cath Maige Tuired she appeared and recited the events and the glory of the dead, before either she or the Morrigan proclaimed two prophecies for the future. In later stories she appears as a stereotypical washer-at-the-ford, washing the clothes or weapons of doomed warriors as an omen of their death (Green, 1992). Before Cu Chulain goes to his final battle he sees a young woman, often identified as Badb, washing bloody clothes and keening (Ó hÓgáin, 2006). The later figure of the Bean Sidhe, considered an omen of death, is linked to Badb and in some dialects of Irish the word badb (pronounced there as bow) is used instead of bean sidhe to describe these beings (Lysaght, 1997).

Banba

Banba, whose name in older Irish means 'place of women's death' is one of the three primary sovereignty goddesses of Ireland along with her sisters Fotla and Eriu (Ó hÓgáin, 2006).

Nearly everything else about her is unclear and contradicted across sources. The Lebor Gabala Erenn gives her mother as Ernmas, but another source lists her as the daughter of Eirnin, and she is said to be the wife of either Etar or Mac Coll (MacKillop, 1998; Macalister, 1944). Similarly, her father may be Daelbeath, Cian, or Fiachra, across various texts (MacKillop, 1998; Banshenchus, n.d.). According to the Foras Feasa ar Eirinn, Banba and her sisters Fotla and Eriu worshipped the Morrigan, Macha, and Badb, while the Lebor Gabala Erenn says all six are sisters.

Her role in myth is no less confusing than her relationships. Ó hÓgáin's *Lore of Ireland* suggests she was the first to settle Ireland, with 150 followers, and the only one to survive the Biblical great Flood by staying in a place on the island that remained above water. This, of course, contradicts her place among the Tuatha Dé Danann who arrived to Ireland much later. Variant texts place her daughter, Cessair, as the first settler of the island instead Ó hÓgáin, 2006).

In the Lebor Gabala Erenn when the Milesians arrive in Ireland, they encounter each of the three sovereignty goddesses in turn, and each extracts a promise that the island will forever bear her name. Banba was used as a poetic name for Ireland, and still remains so although it has fallen out of common use. Despite this it is likely that she was originally a sovereignty goddess specifically for Leinster and Meath, given her close association with Teamhair [Tara] (Ó hÓgáin, 2006).

Bodb Derg

A son of the Dagda and a king of the sidhe. A somewhat obscure figure he appears in a few stories in minor roles, such as the Aislinge Óengusso and De Choppur in Dá Muccida. His name means 'red Bodb' and there has been some suggestion that Bodb and Badb may have originally been a single entity only later differentiated possibly due to scribal errors.

Bóinn

Bóinn is the particular goddess of the river Boyne which bears her name, thought to be from Bó-fhionn meaning white cow. It has been suggested that her name may correlate to the Milky Way, which she could have been associated with (Murphy, 2020). She has strong connections to Brú na Bóinn and the surrounding area. In some sources she is connected to poetry and local folklore that a person who drank from the river Bóinn in June would be granted visions and the gift of poetry (Ó hÓgáin, 2006). In one of the Dindshenchas tales of the river its said that Bóinn went to a sacred well which only Nechtan and his cupbearers were allowed near and when she approached the water surged up three times, injuring her leg, arm, and eye before she fled; the water poured after her and created the river (Ó hÓgáin, 2006; MacKillop, 1998).

Besides the river she is also strongly associated with cattle, especially white cows as her name would indicate. Her connection to specific cows in white, red, brown, and 'dark' may reflect an older connection to the phases of the moon (Smyth, 1988).

In some stories her husband is Nechtan while others name him as Elcmar. Her lover was the Dagda, with whom she had an affair and a child while her husband was away. To cover up the pregnancy the Dagda caused the earth to stand still for nine months, creating the illusion of a single day passing. Their son was Óengus mac ind Óg, who would later come to possess Brú na Bóinn.

Brighid

One of the most popular Irish goddesses in modern times is Brighid, also called Brigid, Brigit, or Bríd in modern Irish and Brig or Bric in older sources. A pan-Celtic goddess, in Ireland she was a deity of healing, fertility, poetry and smithcraft, sometimes seen as a single deity and sometimes as three sister deities all named Brighid; Brighid of the poets, Brighid of the forge, and Brighid the healer. Whether an individual or three sisters, they were daughters of the Dagda. This idea appears in the Sanas Cormaic and possibly reflects a later understanding of the goddess who is usually described as an individual being in other sources where she is more usually connected to poetry. Ó hÓgáin says that Brighid, whose name probably means "Exalted One", is a protector and inspirer of poets, as well as being connected to agricultural fertility. The Sanas Cormaic also says that "among all the Irish a goddess used to be called a Brigit", emphasizing her importance, although again this source should be taken with at least a small grain of salt. The information we have relating to Brighid comes from the older mythology including the Cath Maige Tuired and Lebor Gabala Erenn as well as mythology of the Christian saint of the same name who many believe is a continuation of the Goddess; modern beliefs and practices surrounding Brighid are an amalgam of older pagan sources and newer Christian ones. Much of this is due to the assumption that many of the beliefs and practices surrounding the saint reflect older pre-Christian beliefs originally attached to the goddess, although it is impossible to know this for certain.

Finding anything clear cut in Irish myth is difficult and this is true of trying to sort out Brighid's family. Her father is clearly referenced in most sources as the Dagda; however, no mother is ever given for her. In some recensions of the Lebor Gabala Erenn she is given as the mother of the three gods of Danu, and some people think that she may be the same deity as Danu, although it is impossible to know with certainty if this is so, or only a medieval attempt to reconcile the pagan mythology into a more cohesive system. In the Cath Maige Tuired she was married to the half-Fomorian/half tuatha Dé Danann, King Bres and bore him a son Ruadán; in some stories she also had three sons with Tuireann named Brian, Iachar, and Iucharba although this may result from confusion between her and Danu. Through the Dagda she is the sister of Óengus mac ind Og, Cermait, Aedh, Midhir, Finnbheara, Ainge, and Bodb Derg.

The Lebor Gabala Erenn tells us that Brighid had two oxen and a pig who would cry out *"after rapine had been committed in Ireland"*, which Ó hÓgáin says relates her to domestic animals. He also sees her as a mother goddess; the saint is referred to as the foster mother of Christ and this may well reflect an older feeling that Brighid was motherly to all those who prayed to her or honoured her. Brighid has many strong associations to healing, particularly of livestock, and also to protection and blessing in folk magic charms. Brighid has a special healing well and site at Cill Dara [Kildare] and is associated with water that has healing powers, as well as a special talisman called a brat Bhride (Brigid's mantle or cloak) which is a small piece of cloth left out on Imbolc eve to be blessed by the goddess/saint which would then have healing properties throughout the year.

Cermait

His name is also spelled Cermat, Cermad, Cermaid, or Cearmaid and his epithets include Minbeoil [small or courteous mouthed] and Milbeol [honey-mouthed] (MacKillop,1998; Daimler, 2015). He is also sometimes called Cermait Caem, or Cermait the fair (Gwyn, 1924). It's uncertain what Cermait means but looking at his name and epithets we can gather that he was both handsome and well spoken.

Cermait is the son of the Dagda and as such has many siblings including Óengus, Aedh, Bodb Dearg, Fionnbheara, Ainge, and Brighid. He had three sons Mac Gréine [son of the sun], Mac Coill [son of the hazel], and Mac Cécht [son of the plough] (MacKillop, 1998). These three sons would later avenge their father's death by killing the person who had killed him, an interesting choice since Cermait's death was not permanent. MacKillop suggests that Mac Cécht is another name for Dain Cécht which would make Cermait the father of the healing deity, although sources suggest that the Dagda may be Dain Cécht's father (MacKillop, 1998; Ó hÓgáin, 2006). We have no known spouse for Cermait but we know of at least one lover of his, Buach who was Lugh's wife.

We do not have many myths preserved where see Cermait actively participating in the story but he is referred to in multiple places including the Dindshenchas and Lebor Gabala Erenn along with his brothers Óengus and Aedh specifically. These three seem to have formed a special grouping, along the lines of what we see in other examples of three closely related deities or those with similar purviews who often act or appear together. There is no surviving mythology of these three acting together, however, only references to them grouped together such as we see here in the Metrical Dindshenchas poem Ailech I: "*good sons were attendant at [the Dagda's] side, Cermait the comely, Óengus, and Aed.*"

There are not many places specifically associated with Cermait but one that is, is his birthplace. According to the Rennes Dindshenchas, poem 4 Dindgnai in Broga, Cermait was born in or near the Brugh na Boinn, as we are told that the Brug is: "*The place wherein Cermait of the Honey-mouth, son of the Dagda, was born*". The Metrical Dindshenchas provides slightly more specific directions for the location of this site at the Brug in the poem 'Brug na Bóinde II' where it uses the Paps of the Morrigan, which are located to the west of Sid in Broga as a landmark:

Behold the two Paps of the king's consort here beyond the mound west of the fairy mansion: the spot where Cermait the fair was born, behold it on the way, not a far step.

This would seem to imply that Cermait's birthplace is between the Sid in Broga and Paps of the Morrigan.

One myth where we do see Cermait taking a more active role, is a story that begins with his corpse. In *How The Dagda Got His Staff* we find that Cermait has been killed by Lugh for having an affair with Lugh's wife Buach. In response to this the Dagda has preserved the body and is carrying it throughout the world looking for a way to return his son to life. Eventually the Dagda comes across three brothers bearing three treasures they had inherited from their father; one of these treasures is a staff which can kill with one end and revivify the dead with the other. The Dagda gains the use of the staff and kills the three brothers then revives Cermait. Cermait immediately asks what is going on and then chastises his father for killing the men, getting the Dagda to return the brothers to life as well. After some negotiation the Dagda is given the staff on loan and he and Cermait return to Ireland.

Creidne

Creidne is one of the three gods of skill of the Tuatha Dé Danann along with his brothers Goibhniu the smith and Luchta the carpenter. Creidne's name is of uncertain meaning but he is called Creidne Cerd, Creidne the wright, a type of craftsmen who would work with bronze, brass, or gold. When Nuada lost his arm in the Cath Maige Tuired it was Creidne, according to the Lebor Gabala Erenn, who worked with the physician god, Dian Cécht, to fashion a prosthetic of silver for him with the motion of an organic arm. During the Cath Maige Tuired itself he aided his people by making sword hilts, spear rivets, and bosses and rims for the shields.

Dagda

"Dagda that is a good god that is an excellent god he was of the pagans; because the Tuatha Dé Danann adored/worshiped

him, because he was a god of the world to them, because of the greatness of his power" – Coir Anmann

One of the most well-known gods of the Tuatha Dé Danann is the Dagda. He can be found under many variations of the name and under many by-names, such as Daghdae, Dagdai, Daghdo, Daghdou, Dagdae, Dagdhua, Dagdhae, Dagda Mor, Dagda Donn and Eochaid Ollathair, Ruad Rofessa, Aedh Alainn, Aodh Ruadh Ro-fessa; usually the definitive article "the" is added before Dagda (Gray, 1983; Ó hÓgáin, 2006). The name Dagda itself is an epithet which means "Good God", implying a God good at all things. This name is gained during the Cath Maige Tuired when he promises to do as much as all the other Tuatha Dé have said they will do in the fight (Gray, 1983). His by-names tell us a great deal about him as well: Eochaid Ollathair "Horseman Great-father", Ruad Rofessa "Red-man of great-Knowledge", Aedh Alainn "Fiery Lustrous One". People inclined to look at the Dagda as a more neopagan type Father God should bear in mind the actual connotations of "Good God" as well as the more restricted translation of Ollathair, as there is no direct evidence that he was previously seen as the literal father of the gods, but rather as prolific. In fairness to that view, however, Ó hÓgáin does suggest that the Dagda can be connected to the "Dis Pater" father deity that Caesar claims the Gauls believed they descended from (Ó hÓgáin, 2006). Additionally, the text of the Cath Maige Tuired provides a long list of names for the Dagda, after he is challenged to give a ride to a Fomorian princess and replies that he has a geas preventing him doing so unless she knows his full name. She asks him three times for his name and on the third request he replies:

Fer Benn Bruach Brogaill Broumide Cerbad Caic Rolaig Builc Labair Cerrce Di Brig Oldathair Boith Athgen mBethai

Brightere Tri Carboid Roth Rimaire Riog Scotbe Obthe Olaithbe (Gray, 1983).

In some sources the Dagda is said to be the son of Elatha and he is married to the Morrigan, although he is also known to have fathered at least one child with Bóinn. His children vary by source but are usually given as Óengus mac ind Óg, Cermait, Aodh Caomh, Conan, Midir, Bodb Derg, Ainge, Finnbheara, and Brighid; in one later example Dian Cécht is also said to be his son (Ó hÓgáin, 2006). He has one known child with the Morrigan, a daughter named Adair. His sons often die after trying to obtain a woman who is not available; only Óengus successfully marries the literal woman of his dreams, Caer Ibarmeith. This may connect the Dagda to the concept of passion or of sexual envy, as he himself fathered Óengus on another man's wife. He is also sometimes said to be the brother of Nuada and Ogma (Ó hÓgáin, 2006).

The Dagda is generally described as being a large man, sometimes comically so, with a tremendous appetite and immense capacity. In the Cath Maige Tuired he is given porridge made with 80 gallons of milk as well as several whole sheep, pigs, and goats, and he ate this meal with a ladle large enough to hold two people lying down. Some modern sources describe him as red-haired, possibly relating to the name Ruad Rofessa, and describe his clothing as a short tunic, sometimes obscenely short, based on the description from the Cath Maige Tuired. He is considered to be generous, wise, and bigger-than-life in his appetites (Ó hÓgáin, 2006). He is often described as immensely strong and able to complete great feats such building a fort single-handedly or clearing 12 plains in a single night.

The Book of Lecan states that the Dagda ruled for 80 years as king of the gods after the death of Lugh, but other sources stay that he was killed fighting Ceithlinn at the second battle of Maige Tuired (Smyth, 1988). This is later explained with a story saying that he took a wound in the battle that took 80 years to kill him, but that is clearly an attempt to unify the varying tales into a coherent whole (Ó hÓgáin, 2006). He was said to be a master of Druidic magic and to possesses several magical objects. It was the Dagda who held the cauldron of abundance brought from Murias, one of the four treasures of the Tuatha Dé Danann. He also owned a great club that was so large it had to be dragged on wheels behind him; it is said that one end of the club could kill nine men with one blow, while the other could heal (Berresford Ellis, 1987; Ó hÓgáin, 2006). His horse was Acein (ocean) and the Dagda possessed a harp whose playing changed the seasons. This harp was stolen by the Fomorians at the end of the Cath Maige Tuired and the Dagda along with Nuada and Ogma had to journey to recover it, possibly indicating its importance to maintaining the order of time and the seasons.

The Dagda is associated with Brú na Bóinn and also with a site in Donegal called Grianan Aileach as well as Leighead Lachtmhaighe in Clare, Cnoc Baine in Tyrone and O Chualann in Wicklow (Smyth, 1988; Ó hÓgáin, 2006). It is said that it was the Dagda who delegated each of the sidhe to the Tuatha Dé after their defeat by the Milesians, possibly at Manannan mac Lir's suggestion (Ó hÓgáin, 2006). The Dagda originally lived at Brú na Bóinn but was tricked out of the site by his son Óengus.

Danu

Danu is an obscure figure whose name appears in older texts as Danand or Danann; scholars have theorized that she is a scribal addition to older stories because the form her name appears in is grammatically incompatible. This may be further supported by suggestions by scholars like John Carey that Danann was added to Tuatha Dé later by Christian scribes to differentiate the term from the same one they were using for the Israelites, and that rather than a name Danann may have been intended as a form of the word dán, meaning skill (Carey, 1981). Whether or not this is true Danu has been understood as a goddess for many centuries and worshipped as one by modern pagans for decades. There are two hills in county Kerry named the 'paps of Danu' (Keating, 1857).

It has been suggested that her name is related to other Celtic and Indo-European river goddesses, and has a meaning connected to 'flowing'. There is some added confusion in trying to sort through her potential appearances in Irish mythology because the Fomorians have a progenitor named Domnu and there is another Tuatha Dé Danann figure, a daughter of Flidais, who is named Dinann, and it is sometimes unclear exactly who is being referenced. Some versions of the Lebor Gabala Erenn give her as a daughter of Ernmas and Delbaeth, sometimes confused with the Morrigan, and the mother of Delbaeth's three sons. In the Cét-Cath Maige Tuired she is referred to as the foster mother of the Morrigan, Badb, and Macha, and along with them accompanies the warriors to the battlefield.

Dian Cécht

The primary Irish god associated with physicians, healing, and restoring the body. Dian Cécht was considered the supreme physician of the gods and in the Cath Maige Tuired is described working, along with several of his children, at a well into which the wounded could be placed and from which they would emerge restored. His name may mean "swift traveller" and he is called "the healing sage of Ireland" and "god of health" (Ó hÓgáin, 2006).

His mother is unknown but his father is Esarg; his brothers are Creidne, Goibhniu, and Luchta. He is the father of two other Irish healing deities, Miach and Airmed, along with his sons Cu, Cian, Cethan, Ormiach, and Ochtriuil and his other daughter the poet Etan (MacAlister, 1941). Lugh is his grandson.

Not only a god of active healing but also of the knowledge of healing arts and of healing magic. He is known as a superlative healer of any method and there is an entry in Saint Gall's Incantations that calls on Dian Cécht, showing that he persisted into the Christian period. The healing well of Slaine was created when he placed one of every healing herb into it, and in mythology he is known to heal grievous wounds and cure plagues in the guise of serpents (Ó hÓgáin, 2006). He also, with the aid of Creidne, replaced Nuada's severed arm with a prosthetic of silver that moved like the original and replaced Midir's eye when it was put out.

Ériu

One of the three primary sovereignty goddesses of Ireland, her name may come from an earlier word for 'land' and the modern version, Éire, is the Irish term for the island itself.

Ériu is a daughter of Ernmas, according to the Lebor Gabala Erenn, along with her sisters Banba, and Fotla, and she is also a sister to the Morrigan, Badb, and Macha. The Fomorian, King Elatha with whom she has a son, Eochaid Bres. In a different source her mother is named Einin and her foster father is given as Codal (Ó hÓgáin, 2006). Her husband is named Mac Gréine and her consort in the Banshenchus is said to be Cetar, although it's unclear if the two are the same being or different.

In the Lebor Gabala Erenn when she encounters the Milesians, she offers them the sovereignty of Ireland if her name remains on the island and they agree; however, Donn insults her and suggests the Milesians should only deal with their own gods, after which she foretells his death at sea and promises that none of his descendants will inhabit Ireland, which comes to pass when his ship sinks off the coast. The Banshenchus describes her as 'fierce' and her and her sisters as 'spirited of speech'. It is possible that in various tales where sovereignty appears personified as an otherwise unnamed goddess it is in fact Ériu.

Fotla

Fotla is one of the three main sovereignty goddesses of Ireland, along with her sisters Ériu and Banba. Similar to her sister Ériu her name may be rooted in an older word for land (MacKillop, 1998). Her mother was either Eirnin or Ernmas, depending on the source; if her mother was Ernmas than her other three sisters would be the Morrigan, Badb, and Macha. Her husband was Mac Cécht and she was the consort of Detar, although it's unclear if they are individuals or the same person under different names (Smyth, 1988). In the Lebor Gabala Erenn, Fotla encountered the invading Milesians and promised them sovereignty if her name would be forever on the island; it is still used as a poetic name for Ireland.

Flidais

Flidais is one of the more enigmatic and intriguing of the Irish deities. References to her in mythology are few and lack detail, yet there seems to be something deep and compelling about her. There is some debate about whether she is a historic deity or a literary creation of the later period, although it may be that her shifting character reflects euhemerization of the goddess into a human literary character, rather than a purely literary creation.

Her name may mean "wet one" and she is especially associated with milk and milking; her epithet is foltchaoin "soft haired" (Ó hÓgáin, 2006). Her husband was Adammair in one source and her son, Nia Segamain (Leahy, 1906). In the Lebor Gabala Erenn her children are listed as Arden, Be Chuille, Dinand, and Be Teite and the Metrical Dindshenchas list her as the mother of Fand (Macalister, 1941; Gwynne, 1906). In the Driving of the Cattle of Flidais she appears as a mortal character, the lover of Fergus mac Roich and wife of Ailill Finn (Leabor na h-Uidre, n.d.).

In the Lebor Gabala Erenn Flidais is said to be the owner of magical cattle, and two of her children, Be Chuille and Dinand, are referred to as *"she-farmers"* connecting them to the produce of the earth, with another, Nia Segamain, is mentioned in relation to her cattle (Macalister, 1941; Leahy, 1906). She was said to also have a herd of deer that gave milk like cows, and her herd was made up of both deer and cows (Keating, 1857). She is associated with both domestic cattle and deer, and all animals are said to be her "cattle" (Ó hÓgáin, 2006). During the Táin Bó Cúailgne she supplied milk from her herd once a week that fed the entire army of Connacht, and in the Táin Bó Flidais she was said to have one cow that could feed 300 men from one milking (Leabar na h-Uidre, n.d.). In this story as well, we learn of Flidais's sexual prowess as she alone could satisfy her lover Fergus; without her it would take seven women to do the same (Ó hÓgáin, 2006).

In the Banshenchus she is also connected to negative aspects, specifically fighting and destruction of men. It says: *"Flidais.... Though slender she destroyed young men. She decreed hard close fighting"*. Although this is the only such reference, in the Driving of the Herd of Flidais she is the source of the conflict so perhaps this reflects and aspect of her that can incite violence.

Modern pagans often associate Flidais with the woodlands and with wild animals, partially due to a conflation of Flidais and Artemis, although in mythology she is equally connected to domestic animals. Her nature in mythology seems to be both motherly, with her many children and connection to milk and milking, and also sensual in her role as the lover of Fergus. She also is clearly a deity of abundance and sustenance, who provides for all who rely on her.

There is at least one reference to Flidais as a healer; in the Táin Bó Flidais it is said that she tended to and healed the men wounded in battle. Interestingly this may relate to a more modern folk charm against poison that calls on "Fleithas", a name similar to the modern Irish for Flidais – Fliodhais. This charm refers to the hounds of Fleithas, as well as the three daughters of Fleithas (Wilde, 1991).

Goibniu

Goibniu, or Goibhniu is the Irish God of smithcraft. His name is derived from the word for smith; Old Irish gobha, Modern Irish gabha (Ó hÓgáin, 2006). It is said that he could forge a weapon with only three blows from his hammer (Berresford Ellis, 1987). Goibniu has two brothers, Creidne the wright and Luchta the carpenter, forming a trinity of crafting gods who are referred to as the three gods of skill. The three often work together to forge the weapons of the gods, with each one making a part of the whole. According to the Lebor Gabala Erenn, Dian Cécht was also his brother and they were all sons of Esarg (Macalister, 1941). Indeed, the four are mentioned together at several points in the Lebor Gabala Erenn such as:

In his [Nuada's] company were the craftsmen, Goibniu the smith and Creidne the wright and Luichne the carpenter and Dian Cecht the leech. (Macalister, 1941).

Although we have few surviving myths featuring Goibhniu he was clearly considered a very important deity. During the battle against the Fomorians in the Cath Maige Tuired he made peerless spears that never missed and killed whoever they hit, excluding only himself. We learn the latter fact after Brighid's son by Bres, Ruadán, goes to the forge, takes one of Goibniu's spears and wounds him with it, only to have the smith turn around and kill the would be assassin with the same spear after pulling it free of his own body. Goibniu is taken to Dian Cécht's healing well and recovers.

Goibniu had a special drink, a mead or ale called the fled Goibnenn, that conveyed the gift of youth and immortality to the Tuatha Dé Danann (Ó hÓgáin, 2006). This drink is sometimes called the feast of Goibniu and is said in some sources to cure disease (Monaghan, 2004). He also owned a cow who gave endless milk, connecting him to both healing and abundance (Ó hÓgáin, 2006).

He has an association with healing according to the St. Gall Incantation in which he is invoked to remove a thorn, possible also a reference to healing a battle wound:

> ...*dodath scenn toscen todaig rogarg fiss goibnen aird goibnenn renaird goibnenn ceingeth ass:-*
> *very sharp is Goibniu's science, let Goibniu's goad go out before Goibniu's goad!* (Stokes, 1901)

He is appealed to for protection in some early Irish charms which call on the art of Goibniu (Ó hÓgáin, 2006). This may relate to the idea that the being that created the weapon which caused the injury had power over the injury caused, something that we see in the charms relating to elf-shot.

Goibniu is especially associated with Cork, and in particular with Aolbach [Crow Island] on Beara peninsula (Ó hÓgáin, 2006). He was said to have his forge there and to keep his magic cow in that area. Other folklore associates him with county Cavan and the Iron mountains there (Monaghan, 2004). In later Irish mythology Goibniu became Gobhan Saer, a smith and architect of the Aos Sidhe (Ellis, 1987).

Luchta

Luchta's name appears in a range of ways, including Luchtain, Luchtaine, Luchtine, or Luchtar. He is one of the three gods of skill, along with his brothers Goibniu and Credne, with his specialty being carpentry. In the Cath Maige Tuired he is mentioned as the one making spear shafts and shields for the army. There is little mythology on him and he mostly appears in references with his three brothers.

Lugh

One of the prominent kings of the Tuatha Dé Danan is Lugh, Lug in older Irish. The name is derived from the proto-Indo-European root *leug(h) which most likely means 'to swear an oath' (Ó hÓgáin, 2006). He has several epithets including Lamhfada [long arm], Ildanach [many skilled], and Samildanach [many joined skills]. He is alternately called Mac Céin, son of Cian, or Mac Ethlenn, son of Eithne (MacKillop, 1998). References to him by his mother's name as a patronymic are particularly interesting because that was not common. One of the epithets applied to him in the Lebor Gabala Erenn is 'rind-agach' which Macalister gives as 'spear slaughterous' although 'spear-combative' is a closer translation.

Lugh ruled as king of the Tuatha Dé Danann after Nuada, taking over the kingship just prior to the Cath Maige Tuired when Nuada stepped aside for him and retaining kingship after Nuada was killed in the battle. Nuada did this because Lugh demonstrated his adeptness at every skill and seemed like the best chance to defeat the Fomorians. He was also part of a prophecy, which said that only Balor's grandson – Lugh – could defeat him; Balor was one of the Fomorian kings and he possessed a poisonous eye that would weaken any it looked upon. Before the battle itself we also see him using magical skill to rally his forces and to curse the opposing army (Gray, 1983).

Lugh was the son of the Tuatha Dé Danann, Cian and the Fomorian, Eithne; his paternal grandfather was the physician God, Dian Cécht and his maternal grandfather the dangerous Fomorian, Balor. There had been a prophecy that Balor's grandson would kill him so Balor imprisoned his daughter in a tower; Cian snuck in to meet with Eithne which resulted in triplets. When Balor found the babies, he cast them into the sea where two of them either drowned or were turned into seals, while Lugh was saved and fostered by either Manannan or Tailtiu (MacKillop, 1998). In the Ulster cycle he is said to be the father of the hero Cu Chulainn by King Conchobar's sister, Dechtire, or alternately that Cu Chulainn was born from the reincarnated soul of Lugh's son through her after she spent time in a sidhe. We see Lugh coming to Cu Chulainn's aid in the Tain Bo Cúailgne when the hero is gravely injured, taking him into the sidhe in order to heal him. In myth and folklore Lugh is given four different wives: Buí (possibly another name for the Cailleach), Nás, Echtach, and Englic (MacKillop, 1998). One of these wives was unfaithful and had an affair with the Dagda's son, Cermait, prompting Lugh's vengeful killing of him; this in turn eventually led the three sons of Cermait to seek revenge on Lugh for their father's death.

Lugh is most strongly associated with the festival of Lúnasa, which bears his name, although it is more properly understood as a memorial for his foster mother Tailtiu. According to the Lebor Gabala Erenn, Lugh instituted the games of Lúnasa in honour of his foster mother after she died, clearing the plain that bore her name (MacAlister, 1941). The holiday itself focuses on the celebration of the beginning of the harvest with things like dressing holy wells, horse races, athletic games, and the preparations of special foods. Today many Lúnasa celebrations centre on Saint Patrick as a divine protector of the harvest but it is likely that Lugh originally held this role and was only later replaced when the new religion came in (MacNeill, 1962).

Lugh may be seen as one of the kings of the Otherworld, particularly associated with Teamhair, as he is depicted as such in the story of Baile in Scáile (Smyth, 1988). He is also strongly associated with the founding of different mortal family lines and several different tribes were named after him (Smyth, 1988). Lugh features strongly in many stories and was clearly an important figure. Some scholars suggest that Lugh was an interloper to the Irish pantheon who was only added later and that his mythology reflects this, showing him being born and coming into the crisis between the Tuatha Dé Danann and Fomorians in a way that displaces the existing King Nuada (Ó hÓgáin, 2006).

Lugh possessed one of the four treasures of the Tuatha Dé Danann, said in myth to be either a sword or spear, although it is most often believed to be a spear (Daimler, 2015). It is said that the spear could never lose in battle. In the story Tuath De Danand na Set soim, we are told that this treasure was acquired by Lugh in a city before the gods came to Ireland, a version echoed in less detail in the Lebor Gabala Erenn, although there is another story about how he gained the spear as well. The Oidheadh Chloinne Tuireann tells us that after Lugh's father Cian was killed by the children of Tuireann, Lugh required them to fulfil a series of impossible tasks and in so doing gained his famous spear as one of the items they retrieved for him.

Macha

Macha is one of the Tuatha Dé Danaan who appears in several different places in Irish mythology. She is a daughter of Ernmas, sister to Badb and the Morrigan; these three sisters make up the triple Morrigan according to the Sanas Cormaic. In some sources Macha herself is called Morrigan or given that title (Ó hÓgáin, 2006). Macha appears in different guises in Irish mythology, once as one of the Nemedians, as one of the Tuatha Dé Danann, as a "fairy woman" and as a queen. This last one may or may not represent an actual historic queen or a story about the Goddess; the story itself has many mythic overtones but is not explicitly mythic so it could be taken either way. Scholars do not agree on whether or not all of these appearances are of the same being or of different beings with the same name. We will resent stories of each of them here for the reader to decide.

In the first story, in the Lebor Gabala Erenn, she appears as the wife of Nemed, of the third group to settle Ireland, and in this tale, she dies clearing the plains of Ireland for farming (Macalister, 1941). In alternate versions her husband cleared the land and she died there so he named it for her, or she clears the land and then has a prophetic vision of the death and destruction of the future Tain Bo Cúailgne which causes her to die of a broken heart (Green, 1992). In any case she is linked to the earth and its produce, through her death in exchange for clearing the land for farming. There are several meanings for the word macha in Old Irish including hooded crow, milking yard/field, and field or plain. In modern Irish the word means cattle field or yard, a fine group of cattle in a pasture, or, when added to brea bo, a herd (O Donaill, 1977). The connection of the word to cows and milking as well as fields and pasture may also supports the connection of her as a land goddess and the symbolism of the Nemedian story.

She appears in the Lebor Gabala Erenn among the Tuatha Dé Danann where she is called a daughter of Ernmas and wife of Nuada Agatlamh (MacAlister, 1941; Berresford Ellis, 1987). Her father is Delbaeth and her sisters are the Morrigan and Badb, as well as the sovereignty goddesses Ériu, Banba, and Fotla. In volume IV of the Lebor translation by R. A. S. Macalister, the translator says *"Delbaeth...has three daughters, the famous war-furies Badb, Macha, and Mórrígu, the latter sometimes called Anand or Danand."* (Macalister, 1941). In the Cath Maige Tuired she is killed along with Nuada in the battle but Macalister, in his introduction to Section VII of the Lebor Gabala Erenn, volume IV says that it is logical to believe that this Macha and the Macha of Ard-Macha who curses the men of Ulster (discussed next) are in fact the same deity. At a later point in the text Macalister also posits that Macha was a later addition to the Badb/Morrigan pairing, saying:

Macha, one of the Badb sisterhood, has a certain individuality of her own, and enjoyed a special cult, probably centred at Armagh (Ard Macha), to which she bequeathed her name. Her intrusion into the Badb sisterhood may be a subsequent development, for the genealogies before us seem to suggest an earlier tradition in which Badb and the variously named third member of the group formed a dyad. (Macalister, 1941).

This provides us a variety of interesting information about Macha. We learn that she is the daughter of Delbaeth and Ernmas, and sister to Badb and Anand, one of the three Morrigan. And we learn – according to the Lebor Gabala Erenn anyway – that Macha falls in battle with Nuada at the hand of Balor of the evil eye.

All of this information is supported in the "index to persons" of the Cath Maige Tuired which references her as one of the Tuatha Dé Danann, and agrees with the Lebor Gabala Erenn's parentage. This index also mentions that in the Banshenchus she is listed as one of the Tuatha Dé Danann's magic workers, and that in the Cét-Cath Maige Tuired she acts with her sisters Badb and the Morrigan to use magic against the enemy, specifically by sending rain, fog, and showers of blood and fire upon the opposing army. The Cath Maige Tuired lists the three sisters as ban-draoithe, or Druids (Gray, 1983).

Next, in a story from the Dindshenchas, she appears as a woman of the sidhe who marries a farmer named Crunnchu, and becomes pregnant with twins. He goes to a festival held by the king who is bragging of the speed of his horses. Crunnchu, despite being warned by Macha not to speak of her to anyone else, says that his wife could outrace any horse, and the furious king demands that Crunnchu bring her immediately to race or forfeit his life. Macha begs for a delay as she is in labour, but is denied and forced to race anyway. She wins, collapsing and birthing her twins just past the finish line and curses the men of Ulster with nine days of labour pain in their greatest hour of need for "nine times nine" generations before dying. In some versions of the story she doesn't die, but simply returns to the Otherworld because Crunnchu broke her prohibition, taking her children with her. According to the Dindshenchas, Macha gives birth to a boy and girl named Fir [truth] and Fial [honourable] (Gwynn, 1924). To this day the spot carries her name, Emain Macha, where for a long-time festivals and assemblies were held, especially at Lúnasa (MacNeill, 1962). It is from this story that her associations with horses, childbirth, pregnancy, justice and, again, the produce of the earth – by marrying a farmer – are seen. In this story it is said that Macha's other name is Grian: *"her two names, not seldom heard in the west, were bright Grian and pure Macha"* and *"in the west she was Grian, the sun of womankind."* (Gwynn, 1924). The word Grian itself has multiple meanings including and all relating to the sun; some meanings are given in the eDIL as sun, shining, bright, radiant, and luminary. This may be an attempt by the Dindshenchas to connect Macha and the Fairy Queen, Grian of Cnoc Gréine in county Limerick; if so it's a tenuous link as there are no other references to this or connecting Macha to the sun in anyway. Grian is more often connected to Áine. As already mentioned There seems to be a clear connection between this Macha and the Macha of the Tuatha Dé Danann.

In the final story also appears in the Dindshenchas. She is Macha Mong Ruadh, Macha Red-Hair, daughter of one of three kings who share the rulership of Ireland, each ruling for seven years in turn. This Macha is listed as the 76th ruler of Ireland and said to have ruled around the 4th century BCE (Ellis, 1987). When her father dies, Macha steps up to rule but is challenged by the other two kings who do not want to co-rule with a woman. She battles them and wins, and when her seven years are over, she refuses to step down since she is Queen not by blood but through victory in battle. She marries one of the original three kings, Cimbaeth. The remaining original king dies, leaving five sons who would challenge her, so she goes to them in the appearance of a crone or leper and seduces them one by one, tying them up afterwards and thereby defeating them and enslaving them. Afterwards she forces the five brothers to build her fort at Emhain Macha.

The Sanas Cormaic calls the severed heads of warriors "Macha's nut crop", and refers to her and her sisters as 'raven women' who stir up strife. Macha is particularly associated with Ulster, Ard Macha [Armagh] and Emain Macha [Navan Fort]. Cu Chulainn had a horse named Liath Macha, "grey of Macha", which wept tears of blood before Cu Chulainn's final battle. Horses and crows are animals often linked to her; in Cormac's glossary she is called "Macha the crow" (Green, 1992). Her connection to horses may be a reflection of her role as a sovereignty goddess, with the horse as a symbol of the rulership of the king (Ó hÓgáin , 2006).

Manannán mac Lir

One of the deities that can be found in the mythology of several different Celtic nations is Manannán; called Manannán mac Lir (son of the sea) in Ireland, and Manawydan to the Welsh. His home was said to be the Isle of Man, called Manaw in Welsh and Manu in Irish; Manannán's name clearly derives from this and since this name for the island is a later development Ó hÓgáin posits that Manannán himself and his mythology are later developments as well, likely dating to no earlier than the 3rd century CE (Ó hÓgáin, 2006). The Irish initially borrowed the name from the Welsh, but then added the title "mac Lir" which was then borrowed into the Welsh as "map Llyr" (Ó hÓgáin, 2006). This demonstrates the composite nature of Manannán that has developed over time as the cultures shared mythology back and forth.

Manannán is described as a handsome warrior (Berresford Ellis, 1987). Manannán's wife is Fand, a peerless beauty who at one point had an affair with Cu Chulainn, until Manannán used his magic to make Cu Chulainn forget about her and return to his own wife, Emer. It is said that Manannán travelled to the mortal world to father Mongán, a prince and hero, and under the name of Oirbsiu he may have fathered the Conmhaicne sept of Leinster (Ó hÓgáin, 2006). There are many stories about his various sons and daughters, who are usually treated as minor characters (Ó hÓgáin, 2006). One of his more well-known children is Áine, although some sources list her as his wife.

Manannán was originally said to live on the Isle of Man, a place which was seen as near mythical in Irish stories; later his home shifted fully into the Otherworld, to Emain Abhlac (Ó hÓgáin, 2006). Emain Abhlac is described in rich detail as a sacred place, an island held up by four silver legs or pillars, on which grew magical apples which gave the island its name Emain of the Apples (Ó hÓgáin, 2006). Other names for his domain include Màg Meall (the pleasant plain) and Tír Tairngire (the land of promise) (Ó hÓgáin, 2006). Each of these names and associations reflect the connection between Manannán's realm and the Otherworld.

He was seen as the lord of the waves, to whom the ocean was like a field of solid land, as well as a master magician and God who could control the weather (Ó hÓgáin, 2006). The fish are said to be his livestock, compared to cows and sheep, and the waves themselves are called his horses; his most special horse is Enbharr, 'water foam', who could run over sea as if it were solid land (Ó hÓgáin, 2006). In the story of his meeting with King Cormac mac Art he is described as carrying a golden apple branch that rang with sweet music that could sooth people to sleep or heal the ill and wounded (Ó hÓgáin, 2006). His powers were numerous; he could travel faster than the wind could blow in his magical boat, he could create realistic illusions, and he had a cloak of forgetfulness that would take the memory from a person (Monaghan, 2004). It was this cloak that he used to cause Cu Chulainn to forget Fand in the story of the Serglige Con Chulainn.

Although he was not counted among the Tuatha Dé Danann in stories until the 10th century, it is Manannán who advises the Tuatha Dé to take up residence in the sidhe, and he who assigned each new home (Ó hÓgáin, 2006). Additionally, he gives three gifts to the Tuatha Dé; the féth fiadha, the feast of Goibhniu, and the pigs of Manannán (Ó hÓgáin, 2006). The féth fiadha was either a spell or cloak that allowed the person to become invisible and travel unnoticed. The feast of Goibhniu was a magical feast that kept the gods young and living. And the pigs of Manannán were immortal swine who could be killed and would return to life. Some sources suggest that it was these actions that earned him a place among the Tuatha Dé Danann, although it's also possible that he fills a role as an outsider deity, not fully part of the Tuatha Dé nor fully separate but liminally placed.

Manannán's nature is as mercurial as the sea. When visiting Elcmar at his sidhe he is paid great tribute with rushes laid out before him and a great feast prepared, yet despite the pleasant visit he dislikes Elcmar and acts against him later (Ó hÓgáin, 2006). In the stories of the Fianna, Manannán is often helpful yet also appears at least once to stir strife and create trouble among the warriors (Ó hÓgáin, 2006).

In several sources rushes are mentioned as offerings for him, so it could be safely assumed that rushes were historically sacred to him (Ó hÓgáin, 2006). The sea and waters were also strongly associated with him, and it said in the story of Oirbsiu that when he died a lake burst forth from his grave. He is also strongly associated with horses and apples.

Miach

A healing deity, Miach is the son of Dian Cécht and brother of Airmed, Ormiach, Ochtriuil, Cu, Cenn, Cian, and Etan. No mother is given for him nor do we know anything about his other personal relationships.

In the Cath Maige Tuired, Miach heals Nuada's severed arm with nine days of effort, so that the flesh arm is returned to the king; he does this by carrying the severed arm against his side for three days, against his chest for three days, then for three days he throws bulrushes against it. He is given the silver arm in payment. His father disapproves of this cure and strikes him three time, but he heals himself each time. Dian Cécht strikes a fourth time and Miach dies; after this every healing herb in the world grew up from his grave and Airmed was organizing them when Dian Cécht scattered them. Later in the Cath Maige Tuired, Miach appears, alive, beside his father, Airmed and Ochtriuil healing injured warriors at the well of Slaine. The Lebor Gabala Erenn also includes the story of Nuada's healing and Dian Cécht attacking Miach, but in some versions Miach isn't killed. In the Oidheadh Chloinne Tuireann, Miach and his brother Ormiach heal the eye of Teamhair's doorkeeper by replacing it with one from a cat, although this ends up causing problems for the doorkeeper as the eye is drawn to mice.

Midir

Midir's name probably comes from a term for measuring, and while it is given in modern Irish as Midhir, Ó hÓgáin suggests Mír as a likely alternative. Sources list him variously as either the Dagda's brother or son, and foster father of the Dagda's son Óengus who would be either his brother or nephew. If he is a son of the Dagda then he would have other brothers and sisters including Aed, Cermait, Finnbheara, Bodb Derg, Brighid, and Ainge. He has two wives, Fuamnach and Etain and two daughters Ailbe and Doirind (MacKillop, 1998).

Midir is a more obscure deity but features in the Tochmarc Etain, which tells the story of how he married Etain and the problems his first wife's jealousy caused. In that story Midir loses and eye when he tries to stop a fight between Óengus and Elcmar, but Dian Cécht heals it. Later after Etain has been lost to the human world and reborn into a human life he appears and woos her away from her new husband; the two fly off in the form of swans after she regains her memories.

Morrigan

The meaning of the name Morrigan is uncertain, because a small spelling variance radically changes the meaning and the original spelling is unknown. Spelled as Morrigan it would mean, roughly, nightmare queen – often given as phantom queen – with the term nightmare not referring to the modern concept of bad dreams but the older concept of malicious nighttime spirits. However, if the name is spelled with a sineadh fada over the o, Mórrigan, it becomes great queen.

The name is a title, and also appears as Morrigu, Morrigna, and Morrighan; it is applied not only to a specific singular goddess but also to that deity's sisters, Badb and Macha, and in modern paganism sometimes to the goddesses Fea and Nemain. In the Lebor Gabala Erenn we are told that her father is Delbaeth and her mother is Ernmas, with Badb and Macha as her sisters as well as the sovereignty goddesses Fotla, Banba, and Ériu. The Lebor Gabala Erenn also tells us, in some versions that *"Ernmas had other daughters, Badb, and Macha, and Morrigu, whose name was Anand"* (MacAlister, 1941). This reinforces that Morrigan's name could actually be Anand (Anu) although in yet other versions of that text it is said to be Danand (Danu) leaving her true name an open question (Gray, 1983). She is the wife of the Dagda, and has a daughter by him named Adair, and one son, Meche, by an unnamed father; Meche had three serpents in his heart which could have destroyed all of Ireland so he was killed

(Gray, 1983). In the Silva Gadelica it is said she had 26 daughters and 26 sons who were all warriors (Gray, 1983).

In mythology the Morrigan aids the Tuatha Dé Danann in fighting against both the Fir Bolg by using magic to confound and weaken the enemy when she and Macha and Badb go to Teamhair and rain fire and blood down on the opposing army (Gray, 1983; Ó hÓgáin, 2006). In the Cét-Cath Maige Tuired she goes with the warriors to the battlefield and when it seems like the battle might be lost, she sets up pillar stones so that the Tuatha Dé Danann cannot retreat or flee but must fight. They eventually win the day.

The Morrigan has roles in many myths and stories but one of the most prominent is the Cath Maige Tuired. She appears there initially to incite Lugh to rise up to overthrow the Fomorians who are oppressing the Tuatha Dé Danann. In the same text when Lugh asks what each person will bring to the battle she promises to pursue and kill their enemies. At a yearly meeting with the Dagda a couple weeks before the battle she offers advice on how to prepare for the fight and then says that she will personally attack one of the Fomorian kings with magic and returns later with two palmfuls of his blood as proof she has done as she promised. After the battle she appears and gives two prophecies for the world to come, one peaceful and one destructive.

In the Ulster cycle she is the one who sets the Táin Bó Cúailgne in motion, according to one version of the story, when she steals a cow from a woman of the sidhe of Cruachan and breeds her with the Donn Cúailgne; the resulting calf is later killed by Finnbennach, the Donn Cúailgne's rival, setting back into motion a long running feud between the two who are actually shape changed men of the sidhe. During the Táin Bó Cúailgne she attacks Cu Chulainn while he is battling another champion at a ford, causing him to be grievously injured and also becoming injured herself – she eventually tricks him into giving her his blessing which heals her. At the end of the story, she appears to incite the two armies to fight.

The Morrigan has many guises and appears in many forms across mythology. The most recognizable is probably that of a hooded crow or raven, although in the Táin Bó Regamna she is described as *'én dub'* a black bird, implying perhaps a more general association with any bird that is black. In the Táin Bó Cúailgne she appears in disguise as both a beautiful young woman and a very old crone, as a wolf, and eel, and hornless heifer, showing a range of forms she can assume.

The Morrigan is associated with war, battle, and death, certainly, but also with victory, strategy, magic, and possibly sovereignty. She incites warriors to fight and also terrifies those she has set herself against. Several authors connect her to sovereignty through her connection to cattle and cattle raiding and Ó hÓgáin sees her as a land Goddess.

The sidhe of Cruachan, also sometimes called Uaimh na gCat, in Roscommon is described in the Dindshenchas as "The Morrigan's fit abode" and is the place most strongly associated with her, although there are other locations around Sid in Broga that are connected to her as well.

Nemain

Nemain is a war goddess who appears primarily in the Táin Bó Cúailgne, with only small references elsewhere. In the Lebor Gabala Erenn she is listed, along with her sister Fea, as daughters of Elcmar and as wives of the obscure war god Neit, although elsewhere in the same source Babd and Nemain are listed as his wives. Badb and Nemain are often associated together in ways that have caused some scholars to suggest that they are the same being (MacKillop, 1998). Although today Nemain is often listed as one of the three Morrigan she is never mentioned as such in older mythology and is clearly listed as distinct from the three Morrigans, although she does often appear with Badb.

Macalister suggests that Fea and Nemain represent a very old twin pairing which was later subsumed into Badb and Nemain, while Heidja suggests that Nemain may be Badb's name, with Badb working as a title. Like Badb her main epithet is Derg, giving us red Nemain.

In stories where she does appear Nemain is associated with madness and battle frenzy. Her name may be connected to the word for venomous or frenzy, and O'Clery's glossary describes her name as meaning fury or terror while the Sanas Cormaic calls her poisonous. Most references to her mention war or battle, and often madness.

Nuada

Green suggests that Nuada's name may mean "cloud-maker" and suggests that his counterparts in other cultures include Nodens, Nudd/Ludd, and possibly the Germanic Tyr (Green, 1992). The arguments put forth to connect the deities etymologically are reasonably sound, relying on the shared reconstructed Indo-European roots of 'noudont' or 'noudent' which means "to catch" and proto-Indo-European root 'neu-d' which means "to acquire" or "to utilize" (Nodens, 2012). However, as with anything involving reconstructed language, it is still only theoretical. There also seems to be a fairly strong mythological connection between these deities, particularly around the loss of an arm and replacement of the limb with one of silver.

Nuada was the king of the Tuatha Dé Danann when they first came to Ireland; in the Lebor Gabala Erenn it is said that he ruled for seven years before the Tuatha Dé came to Ireland, was displaced when he lost an arm in battle, and then ruled a further 20 years after being healed (Macalister, 1941). Nuada was the son of Echtach, and had four sons, Tadg, Caither, Cucharn, and Etaram the poet, as well as a daughter Echtge; no mother is mentioned (Gray, 1983). It has been suggested that he was married to Macha, one of the three Morrignae, and he possessed one of the four treasures brought to Ireland by the Tuatha Dé, a sword which once unsheathed no enemy could escape and no wound from it could be healed (Berresford Ellis, 1987, Ó hÓgáin, 2006; Jones, 2012). Ó hÓgáin suggests that his name may mean "catcher" and theorizes that Nuada is the same deity as Nechtan and Elcmar (Ó hÓgáin, 2006). He suggests this based on another name for Nuada being Nuada Necht, which Ó hÓgáin believes is the earlier form of Nechtan; by this association Nuada would have been the original owner of Brú na Bóinn and would also possess the source of the Boyne, the well of Nechtan. Other sources also suggest Nuada being the same deity as Nechtan and Elcmar, making him the husband of Bóinn who is cuckolded by the Dagda and then tricked out of possession of the Brú by Bóinn and the Dagda's son from the affair, Óengus (Monaghan, 2004). Based on this idea it would appear that after losing the Brú to Óengus Nuada moved to Sidhe Chleitigh, although alternate stories later claim his home to be sidhe Almhu or Slievenamon (Green, 1992; Monaghan, 2004; Ó hÓgáin, 2006).

Nuada's most well-known epithet is Airgetlamh, silver hand or arm. His name also appears as Nuadha, Nuadae, Nuadai, and Nuodai, with alternate spellings of his epithet as Aircetlaum (Gray, 1983). In the story of the Cath Maige Tuired Nuada was said to have lost his arm in battle, after which Dian Cécht, with the help of the smith Creidne, fashioned him a new arm of silver that looked and moved just as a real arm would (Macalister, 1941). According to a note by Gray in the *Index to Persons of the Cath Maige Tuired* there is a story where Nuada's severed arm is carried off after the battle by a hawk (Gray, 1983). Because of this disfigurement Nuada was forced to forfeit his kingship, for the law of the Tuatha Dé Danann stated that only an unblemished king could rule (Monaghan, 2004; Macalister, 1941). Ó hÓgáin suggests, in his book *The Lore of Ireland*, that the original story of the loss of Nuada's arm may have actually involved an accident with his own sword, or even an intentional sacrifice, and that there may have been some connection to healing waters or even that his lost arm may have been symbolic of a river (Ó hÓgáin, 2006). During the medieval period the story was expanded to include more details; it was his right arm that was lost in battle with the Fir Bolg warrior Sreng (Ó hÓgáin, 2006; Gray, 1983). Nuada was carried from the field only to return the next day with the request that Sreng tie his own right arm to ensure fair combat – when Sreng refused the other Tuatha Dé Danann offered a province of land to keep Nuada from risking his life in an unequal fight (Gray, 1983; Ó hÓgáin, 2006). At this point Bres became king, and Dian Cécht fashioned the silver arm, then after seven years his son Miach, possibly along with Ormiach, replaced it with an arm of flesh and Nuada took back the kingship, beginning the Cath Maige Tuired (Macalister, 1941; Monaghan, 2004; Ó hÓgáin, 2006). During the battle Nuada gives the kingship to Lugh, who organizes the battle and fights the fearsome Fomorian, Balor, who is Lugh's grandfather (Green, 1992). By some accounts Nuada ruled for 20 years after being healed, while others state that he and Macha died together in the Cath Maige Tuired at the hand of Balor (Gray, 1983; Macalister, 1941).

Nuada is a complex deity who can be seen as a god of battle, war, and also justice (Gray, 1983). Some sources also connect him to hunting (Jones, 2012. If weight is given to the parallels between Nuada and the British Nodens and to the possible connections to Nechtan and Elcmar then he could also be seen as a god of healing and of the water, particularly rivers. The sword would be one of his symbols, as he possessed the sword that was one of the four treasures, and hawks may be associated with him. As Nechtan he would be connected to salmon through the salmon of knowledge that lived at the source of the river Boyne.

Óengus

Óengus, also spelled Aengus, is one of the most prominent sons of the Dagda, and features in several significant stories. In De Gabail in t-Sida we are told of how the Dagda wanted to take Bóinn as his lover, but she was married to Elcmar. To solve this conundrum the Dagda, who was king of the Tuatha Dé, sent Elcmar off on an errand then met with Boinn. The two conceived a son, Óengus, and to hide this the Dagda caused the day to last for nine months, so that the pregnancy and birth all occurred in a single 'day'. Óengus's name means unique power and his most common epithet is some variant of mac ind Óg which can be read as the son of the youths or son of the young ones.

In another main story of Óengus the Tuatha Dé have gone into the sidhe and each has been assigned a dwelling place except for Óengus. On the advice of his foster-father he goes to the Dagda whose residence is at Sid in Broga [Newgrange] and requests that he be given the place for a day and a night. The Dagda grants this request but when he returns the next day Óengus refuses to leave, stating that all of time passes in a day and night and that was the amount of time he was given. The Dagda accepts that he has been successfully tricked and leaves. In an interesting turn which again demonstrates Óengus's cleverness, in the Cath Maige Tuired the Dagda is forced to work for the unfit King Bres and while doing so is mistreated by the satirist Cridenbel. When Óengus learns of this he gives his father a plan to free himself from the satirist without any consequences, which is carried out and works perfectly.

The Aislinge Óengusso is the story of Óengus, eventually, meeting his literal dream woman. Óengus starts to be visited at night by a mysterious woman who disappears at dawn and shortly afterwards falls into a love-sickness. He consults a physician who brings in his mother and eventually his father for aid, but they are all unable to help find the woman. Finally, the

Dagda reaches out to Bodb Derg, another of his sons and a king of a specific sidhe, who finds the identity of the young woman; she is Caer Ibormaeth and she spends a year in the form of a woman with her attendants then they all spend a year as swans. Óengus goes to the lake they are at and approaches Caer who eventually accepts him and the two fly off together as swans.

Drawing on the symbolism in the Aislinge Óengusso and the connection to Sid in Broga, Anthony Murphy has suggested that there might be a deeper alignment with the constellation of Cygnus. This connection draws on the various myths, the alignment of Sid in Broga and Fourknocks, the habitual wintering of swans in the area, and the connection between Fourknocks and the constellation Cygnus, and the shape of the mound to suggest that the myths and monuments are connected to the constellation. While only speculation at this point it adds a fascinating layer to Óengus's story.

Ogma

Ogma lends his name to the writing system known as the Ogham. His epithets are Grianeces [sun poet] and Grianainech [sun faced] although it should not be read too literally as sun was used in terms like these as an adjective somewhat equivalent to the English 'sunny'. Ogma's father is Elatha and his brothers are given as the Dagda, Bres, Delbaeth, and Elatha. His wife is the poet Etan and his children are Tuireann, Delbaeth, and Cairpre (Macalister, 1944). He is often listed as one of the three champions of the Tuatha Dé Danann along with the Dagda and Lugh. In the Cath Maige Tuired, Ogma is the champion that Lugh must defeat to prove his own value as a champion and in that same story in the fight against the Fomorians, Ogma promises to defeat kings and much of the opposing army, and indeed in the battle he engages on of the main Fomorian kings in combat.

He possess a special sword, named Orna, which relates everything that has been done with it when it's drawn from its sheath (Sjoestedt, 2000). In general, Ogma is associated with both physical and verbal prowess, and is seen as a god of warriors and poets.

Chapter 9

Other Spirits

"The three dark places of Ireland: the cave of Knowth, the cave of Slaney, the cave of Ferns."

— Triads of Ireland

While the most familiar Irish gods may be the Tuatha Dé Danann, those are not by any means the only ones. In this chapter we will look at some of the other beings found in Irish myth and folk belief, both as general groups and by name.

Fir Bolg

Like the Tuatha Dé Danann, the Fir Bolg are also descendants of Nemed and the third wave of settler to Ireland. According to myth the Fomorians put the Nemedians under terrible oppression and some of them left to later become the Tuatha Dé Danann while others travelled to Greece[16] and came to be known as Fir Bolg, men of the bags. Facing terrible conditions in their new home they eventually left to return to Ireland as the fourth wave of settlers, taking over the now empty island.

Before the eventual arrival of the Tuatha Dé Danann the Fir Bolg king, Eochaid, had a vision of a flock of black birds arriving on the island which his druid interpreted as a warning. Soon after the Tuatha Dé arrived and the two groups fought for dominance of Ireland. Although the Tuatha Dé emerged victorious, the Fir Bolg champion, Sreng, badly wounded the Tuatha Dé King, Nuada, and to prevent him from being killed the Fir Bolg were offered the province of Connacht. The Fir Bolg, Tailtiu, would later act as a foster mother to the god Lugh, and the holiday of Lúnasa was instituted in her honour after her death, showing that the relationship between the two groups was complex.

Fomorians

A significant group of beings who appear repeatedly throughout Irish myth, the Fomorians are often antagonists in stories and viewed as chthonic powers but also share close ties with the Tuatha Dé Danann. Fomorian has sometimes been interpreted as coming from fo muir, under the sea, and the name has been translated in stories as sea-pirate. The Fomorians occupy an interesting liminal space, being both deeply connected to Ireland and also perpetually foreign to it; they put both the Nemedians and Tuatha Dé Danann under tribute, requiring exorbitant taxes be paid to them but are also connected via both Bres and Lugh directly to the Tuatha Dé's kingship. Bres, the unfit king who is the cause of the second Cath Maige Tuired, is the child of a Tuatha Dé mother and a Fomorian father, while Lugh, the Tuatha Dé king that leads his people to win against the Fomorians, is the son of a Fomorian mother and Tuatha Dé Danann father. The Dagda takes an unnamed Fomorian princess as a lover, again showing that the two groups are not entirely antagonistic to each other.

In more recent folklore the Fomorians are described as hideously ugly and sometimes deformed, although Bres's Fomorian father is described in the Cath Maige Tuired as exceptionally beautiful. Nothing with the Fomorians is clear cut or straightforward.

Crom Cruach

Crom Cruach, synonymous according to scholars with Cenn Cruiach, and likely also the same as Crom Dubh (Smyth, 1988; Ó hÓgáin, 2006; MacNeill, 1962). Crom means bent, stooped or crooked; cruach has a wider array of meanings including stack of corn; rick; heap, conical pile, gory, bloody; high-coloured; bloodthirsty, slaughter, wounding, carnage (eDIL, n.d.). The meaning of Crom Cruach's name is uncertain but many people seem to read it as either "bent bloody one" or "crooked heap". Cenn Cruiach may mean "head of the hill" (MacNeill, 1962). Crom Dubh may mean "Black stooped one" or "dark croucher" and Daithi Ó hÓgáin believes all the different iterations of Crom are actually derived from Christian imagery of the anti-Christ and that the deity himself is a later literary invention (Ó hÓgáin, 2006). In contrast, Daragh Smyth sticks with the suggestion from the source material that Crom was the primary God of the pagan Irish before the conversion (Smyth, 1988).

In modern folklore many Lunasa celebrations centre on the defeat of Crom by saint Patrick, often on the last Sunday in July or first in Sunday August which is called Domhnach Chroim Duibh – "Crom Dubh Sunday" (Smyth, 1988). Marian MacNeill believes that these stories likely reflect older pagan tales which would have seen Lugh battling against Crom, with Lugh securing the harvest for the people (MacNeill, 1962). Through this understanding Crom at Lunasa represents the primal force that is either trying to steal the harvest or keep the harvest and with whom a hero must contend to secure supplies for the community. Many of the myths relating to Lugh and Crom Dubh, who is sometimes called Crom Cruach, involve Lugh battling and outwitting Crom and thus ensuring the safety and bounty of the harvest; in some cases, this theme is given the additional layer of the defeat, sacrifice, consumption, and then resurrection of Crom's bull which may argue for an older element of bull sacrifice on this day (MacNeill, 1962). Several scholars, including MacNeill and Smyth suggest a possible connection between Crom and Lugh's Fomorian grandfather Balor. According to this theory Crom is in fact Balor by another name, and the story of Saint Patrick and Crom Cruach battling over the harvest is a thinly disguised version of an older tale of Balor and Lugh's combat.

Besides Lunasa Crom is strongly associated with Samhain when it was said he was honored at Mag Slecht with offerings of the firstborn of every living thing in exchange for a good harvest of corn and milk. According to the Rennes Dindshenchas three-quaters of the people who bowed down to him died.

In modern Irish paganism those who worship Crom see him as a primordial harvest god, and view him as a guardian of the harvest or god of the grain without the negative connotations of the mythic material. Through this lens he is often also understood as one of the primary pre-Celtic pagan deities, although there is, of course, no way to prove that with any certainty.

Cailleach

The Cailleach is a fascinating and mysterious being who may have roots in neolithic Ireland or may be one of the Tuatha Dé Danann under a different name. Cailleach itself, caillech in older Irish, is a word that was borrowed in from Latin, and meant veiled one, used both for nuns and older women; later it came to take on meanings of hag or witch. There are several Cailleachs found in Ireland but the most prominent is the Cailleach Beara, named for the Beara peninsula in Cork where she is thought to live. She is also sometimes called the Cailleach Béarrach in folklore, a word that means sharp or horned, possibly a connection to cattle. In a 9th century poem 'The Lament of the Old Woman of Beare' we are told the Cailleach's name is Buí, a word that means yellow, although it's possible that the name was originally Boí, meaning cow, which might be a reference to her role as a sovereignty goddess (Murphy, 1956; Ó hÓgáin, 2006). This connection to cattle is somewhat supported by her legendary possession of a powerful bull, the Tarbh Conraidh, who had only to bellow to get a cow with calf. In contrast, MacKillop suggests that she her original name may have been known Dígde, a sovereignty goddess of Munster, and that she may also be connected to Duineach, both of which he theorizes were subsumed into the single identity of the Cailleach Beara at some point (MacKillop, 1998).

She is considered a sovereignty figure, credited with creating many of the standing stones and geographic features in various areas, who folklore claims are people or animals that she transformed; her bull the Tarbh Conraidh, for example, was turned into a stone in a river by her when he tried to swim across it to reach a herd of cows on the other side. It is said in county Meath that the Sliab na Cailligh were created when the Cailleach dropped stones over the area as she passed by (Smyth, 1988). Cairn T at this site also has a large roughly chair shaped stone known as the Hag's Chair near the backside of the cairn. Leaba Chaillí, the Hag's Bed, in Cork is a wedge tomb associated with her, where local folklore claims she both lived and was buried. She is associated with a standing stone, the Hag's Stone or the Cailleach Bheara [hag of Beara], resting above Coulagh Bay, Cork. The story is that the Cailleach was Manannán's wife and she turned to stone waiting on shore for him to return from the sea. Some say that the stone is her face, still looking out at the water. The stone is on a steep hillside but can be reached by following a narrow path. It is visited by people who leave offerings on and around the stone.

In other parts of Ireland including Connacht, Leinster, and Ulster the Cailleach Beara is seen as the spirit of the harvest who inhabits the grain and flees from the scythes in the form of a hare (Ó hÓgáin, 2006). In many areas harvest traditions included the practice of leaving the final sheaf standing in the field and naming it the Cailleach, or of dressing the final sheaf as an image of the goddess. In some cases, this sheaf is kept through the winter.

The Cailleach may be connected to the Tuatha Dé Danann if her name is Buí, who is said to be a wife of Lugh. She is generally described as an older woman but she also can appear young, and is considered the ancestor of some family lines including the Corca Duibhne (Smyth, 1988). A tenth century poem says that she was the lover of the warrior Fothadh Canainne. Folklore claims that she has two sisters, also named Cailleach of their respective areas, who live in Dingle and Iveragh (Ó hÓgáin, 2006).

In the Cailleach we see a complex and ancient deity, perhaps rooted in pre-Celtic belief but certainly once a powerful sovereignty goddess. It was she who created several features of the landscape of Ireland making her cosmogonically significantly. The Cailleach may appear old or young, and may give sovereignty to kings, even divine kings if we see her as Lugh's wife and the source of his legitimacy as king of the Tuatha Dé Danann. Although she is often considered a more obscure deity today, and her place among the Tuatha Dé Danann is somewhat uncertain, she seems to have been very significant historically and certainly maintains a powerful place in folklore today.

Donn

There is some debate about whether the Irish have a God of the dead, but if they do its generally agreed that it would be Donn, a king of the Milesians, who died at sea when the sons of Mil were trying to take Ireland. The place where he died, off the southwest coast of Ireland, was called Tech Duinn – Donn's house. Tech Duinn became equated in folklore with the Otherworldly land of the dead and Donn with a primal ancestor and underworld God (Jones, 2004). In the Death Tale of Conaire, Donn is explicitly called the King of the Dead and a 9th century text has Donn claiming that all who die will go to him and his house (Ó hÓgáin, 2006).

According to Green, Donn's name means 'Dark One', however, looking up the Old Irish we see a variety of meanings for the word donn including brown, noble, poet, stolen property, pregnant, and ale (Green, 1997; eDIL, n.d.). The dictionary also defines Donn as:

> *Probably the god of the dead or the ancestral father to whom all are called at their death; Amalgamated with the Christian Devil* (eDIL, n.d.).

Both Green and Jones compare Donn to the Roman Dis Pater, who Caesar said the Gauls believed they descended from; as Donn was seen to be an ancestor of the Milesians and also a deity of the land of the dead this comparison seems valid. Green goes further in saying that Donn is likely also Da Derga, who appears according to her as a death god in the story of Da Derga's Hostel (Gren, 1997). Berresford Ellis suggests that Donn might also relate to Dagda and Bile (Ellis, 1987). Ó hÓgáin agrees with the Dagda association, seeing the name Donn as originally an epithet most likely of an Dagda's; he relates the name to the concept of darkness and the realm of the dead (Ó hÓgáin, 2006).There are a variety of explanations for why Donn died. I have heard some Irish pagans say that it is because he insulted Eriu, one of the main sovereignty goddesses of Ireland, when the Milesianas were negotiating with her. Others say Eriu only predicted his doom but did not cause it (Berresford Ellis, 1987). The actual text from one redaction says:

> *Then Donn son of Mil said: I shall put, said he, under the edge of javelin and sword all that are in the island now, only let land be reached. The wind concentrated upon the ship where Donn the king was, and Donn was drowned at the Sandhills; whence Tech Duinn derives its name* (Macalister, 1944

I tend to read this myself and believe that it was his threat to kill all living things in Ireland that led to the sea and air turning against him and causing his death before his ship could land.

Folklore tells us that Tech Duinn is a place where the dead go, but not necessarily their final destination. Some believe that the house of Donn is where the dead go before moving on to the Otherworld (Berresford Ellis, 1987). In the 8th to 10th centuries Tech Duinn was seen as an assembly place of the dead, and a place that the dead both went to and left from (Ó hÓgáin, 2006). Besides Tech Duinn (present day Bull Rock, County Cork) Donn is also connected to Cnoc Firinne in county Limerick and Dumhcha in county Clare.

The Donn of Cnoc Firinne had strong aspects of a lord of the Aos Sidhe, being called Donn Firinne and said to kidnap people into his hill who had been thought to have died (Ó hÓgáin, 2006). Like many other Irish deities, belief in Donn seems to have survived conversion to Christianity by shifting him from god to good neighbor, albeit a very powerful one. In county Clare Donn was Donn na Duimhche, Donn of the Dune, and was believed to ride out as a fairy horseman with his army (Ó hÓgáin, 2006).

Donn may or may not always have been seen as a deity but he certainly seems to have been understood as one from at least the 8th century onward, until his shift into an Otherworldly horseman. throughout his shifting mythology though, he has always been related to death and the dead, both as the Lord of the 'house' where the dead go and also as a primordial ancestor of the people. He also has a strong association to the sea, the drowned, and to horses.

Tailtiu

Tailtiu was a queen of the Fir Bolg, the fourth group to arrive in Ireland. According to myth the Fir Bolg were descendants of the people of Nemed, the third settlers of Ireland, who fled oppression by the Fomorians. She gave her name to Tailtiu

[Telltown] in Meath and Telton in Roscommon (eDIL, 2024). Her father is sometimes said to be Mag Mór [great plain] or Umor Mór, and some claim he was the king of Spain (MacKillop, 1998). Her husband is the Fir Bolg king, Eochaid mac Eirc, and her foster son was Lugh, who was placed in her care by his father Cian after being rescued from Balor (Smyth, 1988).

In the Lebor Gabala Erenn we are told that she died clearing the plains in Meath for cultivation and as she was dying asked her foster son Lugh to memorialize her with yearly games. This was the institution of the harvest festival of Lúnasa, discussed in Chapter 5.

Tlachtga

Tlachtga is an obscure figure associated with a hill which bears her name. It is unclear which, if any, of the spirit people she might belong to but she is acknowledged as a goddess today. According to the Dindshenchas, her father was Mug Rotha [Servant of the Wheel] and her brothers were Búan [Enduring] and Corb. With her father and a character named Simon Sechtmisid she helped fashion a fantastic wheel device. Unfortunately, she was assaulted by Simon's three sons and died birthing the triplets conceived through them.

Samhain celebrations at Tlachtga [Hill of Ward] in Athboy are thought to stretch back to antiquity and are still celebrated today.

Aos Sidhe

The Aos Sidhe [people of the Otherworldly hills] are a fascinating group of beings found in mythology and through to modern belief. In mythology they exist as a separate and distinct group from the Tuatha Dé Danann, although the latter would later go into the sidhe and join them. In stories set prior to that happening we see the Tuatha Dé and we also see references to the "Riders of the Sidhe", particularly in the Cath Maige Tuired where the phrase is used in connection with the Fomorians and in the Oidheadh Chlainne Tuireann where it is used for a third faction allied with the Tuatha Dé against the Fomorians. Myth also tells us that Manannán was a king of the Otherworld, specifically of an Otherworldly island called Emain Abhlac, and that he taught the Tuatha Dé how to live in the sidhe after the Milesians arrived in Ireland. The fact that the Aos Sidhe were originally a distinct group but were merged with the Tuatha Dé Danann later causes a lot of confusion, especially as the various named Tuatha Dé were often considered kings or queens of their respective sidhe. While it would be best to understand the Tuatha Dé Danann today as part of the Aos Sidhe it would also be good to understand that the Aos Sidhe are comprised of more than just the Tuatha Dé and that there are members of the sidhe who are not and never were Tuatha Dé.

The name Aos Sidhe comes from the belief that these beings dwelt within the Otherworldly hills, or that those hills served as entrances to their Otherworldly realm, which was sometimes located on or in a hill but could also be in a lake or cave. The Aos Sidhe were equally likely to be connected to Otherworldly islands, usually seen in the west, which fisherman occasionally glimpsed out on the water but could never reach, as to the hills and mounds (McNeill, 1959). In Irish lore the Fair Folk live in the land, on the sea, and in the air, being associated with the mounds, stone circles, watery locations including the sea and bogs, caverns, and strange swirls of wind, as well as specific trees, especially lone Hawthorn trees (Ó hÓgáin, 2006). These Otherworldly lands are described as being fair beyond measure, beautiful, peaceful, and rich, and many mortals in tales who were taken into the Otherworld did not want to leave it until a longing to see their families or old homes finally over took them. Generally, when such people did leave this realm, they would find that hundreds of years had passed and they themselves would die as soon as they touched mortal earth, because time moves differently in the Otherworld. This is illustrated in the tale of Niamh and Oisin, where the sidhe woman, Niamh, appears to the Fianna warrior, Oisin, Fionn mac Cumhal's son, and offers to take him to the Otherworldly island of Tir na nÓg, the Land of the Young. Oisin is smitten by the woman and goes with her, but after several years pass, he longs to see his family and the Fianna again; Niamh eventually agrees but on the condition that he not set foot on the ground. She loans him a magical horse who can cross water as easily as land and he travels back to Ireland only to find that everything has changed and no one remembers him or knows his family anymore except as legend. He ends up falling to the ground when the saddle slips as he tries to help a group of men move a rock, and as soon as he touches the ground three hundred years catch up to him.

The Aos Sidhe are not limited in any way to the Otherworld or to the area around the earthly entrances to their realm. In many stories they fare forth into our world, even appearing in mortal markets and fairs. Often, they go unrecognized in such places, unless someone with the second sight sees them or they encounter someone who has previously dealt with them and still retains the ability to see them. In stories of borrowed midwives, the midwife is often given a salve to rub on the new baby's eyes (usually after delivering the child from a local girl thought dead but actually taken by the Good Folk) and accidentally dabs a small amount on her own eye, only to have it put out later when she sees and greets the Otherworldly father at a public market. Likewise, we see stories of various Queens of the sidhe who take mortal lovers, often permanently, and of kings, like Finnbheara, who enjoy watching mortal horse races, showing their both their interest in the human world and ability to move around in it.

Between the different sidhe – of which there are many – exist fairy roads and paths which are invisible to mortal eyes and on which the Fair Folk travel; people must not build on these roads because to build a house on a fairy road inevitably leads to ill-luck and often death (Ó hÓgáin, 2006). To disturb the earthly site of the aos sidhe's home was never a good idea either. Whether it was digging into a mound or cutting down a fairy tree, misfortune and possibly death was sure to follow (Ó hÓgáin, 2006). This belief is so pervasive and strong that to this day people will protest road planning if it interferes with known fairy trees or mounds.

The Aos Sidhe, also called the Daoine Sidhe, both meaning people of the Otherworldly hill, are often referred to with euphemisms like Daoine Eile [Othercrowd], Daoine Uaisle [Noble Folk], Daoine Maithe [Good Folk], and na hUaisle [Gentry]; sometimes they are called fairies in English or siógaí in Irish. In the older belief it was thought to be bad luck to call the Daoine Sidhe by that name, or any name using "sidhe", but this prohibition has shifted to the term fairies, so that now it is considered bad luck to call them fairies as it may offend them. In modern practice many people have a strong prohibition against referring to them by any form of sidhe or using the word fairy, sticking instead to euphemisms (Ó hÓgáin, 2006). In some contexts it is difficult not to use terms the majority of people are familiar with, so sometimes cautious compromises must be made; however, it should be remembered that the Irish Aos Sidhe are in no way the same as the modern conception of fairies, being human-sized, wingless, and decidedly not spirits of nature. In some cases, they are also referred to as wee folk or little people, likely something that began as a way to minimize their power or influence but has come to reflect a belief by some that their physical stature has literally shrunk, reducing them to child-sized beings.

The Aos Sidhe are described in some folklore as slightly taller than humans and very beautiful, while other sources describe them as looking much like humans but with an Otherworldly aura about them. Generally, the people of the fairy hills might have a slight glow to them and were usually finely dressed, but otherwise were very human-like in appearance (Ó hÓgáin, 2006). In folklore they often appear wearing green or grey, and may be blond or brown haired; they might be male or female and can appear alone or in groups. Among the Irish sidhe women were known to appear with messages or warnings, while groups of sidhe men would show up to play games of hurling, for which they required a single human player in order to have the game (Yeats, 1966). The Daoine Sidhe were also known to ride out in processions, especially at Samhain and Bealtaine when they moved their homes, which could be dangerous to any humans they came across. The Fair Folk are usually invisible to mortal eyes, unless they wish to be seen or the person has a special ability to see them, but their passing can sometimes be perceived nonetheless. The fairy host travelling may create whirlwinds or sudden blasts of wind called sidhe gaoithe or séideán sídhe (MacKillop, 1998). This ability to seem invisible is a hallmark of the Aos Sidhe which is mentioned even in mythology; in the Lebor Gabala Erenn we are told the Tuatha Dé Danann learn to pass invisibly after going into the sidhe, in the Táin Bó Cúailgne a man of the sidhe crosses a battlefield unseen, and in a story called the Altram Tige Dá Medar a woman adopted by the Aos Sidhe is separated from them while in the mortal world and loses her ability to see them while becoming visible to the humans around her. This ability, sometimes called the feth fiadha, is seen in almost all stories of the sidhe and goes beyond simply granting invisibility; in many stories it creates a full sensory illusion, for example, a desolate cave is made to look like a castle or a handful of leaves made to appear as gold coins but these things also smell and feel and sound like the they look, in spite of their actual nature.

In mythology and folklore, the Aos sidhe have been known to both marry and produce children with a human, although with the Aos sidhe they seem more likely to steal a bride from her wedding to marry one of their own number instead, who would later be helped by a borrowed midwife to deliver her Otherworldly husband's child. It is generally believed that the Daoine Sidhe have a low birth rate and need to supplement their numbers, which they do with human babies and women; they are also well known to take midwives and musicians, although those are usually released after a time back to our world. Those taken into a sidhe could not return if they ate or drank anything while there, unless they had been given the food by a queen or king fo the sidhe, with whom this rule didn't seem to apply. There are also stories of those who join the Daoine Sidhe for what they think will be a single night of dancing or entertaining in a sidhe and emerge at dawn to find that seven, 70, or hundreds of years have passed on earth. The Fair Folk were also well known for stealing cattle and horses that they fancied (Ó hÓgáin, 2006).

The various sidhe were seen as being deeply territorial and often had rivalries with sidhe from other provinces. McNeill writes about beliefs anchored around Lúnasa that the Aos Sidhe would wage great battles or play games of skill to see whose province or territory would have the better harvest, and that these battles sometimes were experienced as storms. We see a similar idea echoed in the De Choppur in Dá Muccida where two sidhe swineherds from different provinces engage in a contest to see who will have the better pigs at the end of each season only to eventually devolve into direct rivalry.

It is believed that Good Folk have white blood and that when two opposing groups battle at night, they might leave otherwise inexplicable white liquid (fairy blood) to be found as evidence of these events in the morning (Ó hÓgáin, 2006). It is widely believed that the Daoine Sidhe are ruled by a monarchy, but they also encompassed a working class who might go to human markets in disguise or appear to human farmers seeking to borrow something, showing the complexity of the culture found within the sidhe (Ó hÓgáin, 2006). The Fair Folk ride on fine horses and are seen in the company of hounds; usually these animals are either black, white, or grey and are said to be the finest possible examples of each animal (Wilde, 1991). In some stories it is said the deer of the forest are the cattle of the fairies (McNeill, 1959).

In folklore the Daoine Sidhe are seen as being especially active on the quarter days, Samhain, Imbolc, Bealtaine, and Lúnasa. It was believed that on these days the fairies moved house, processing forth from one hill to another along set fairy roads (McNeill, 1956). Samhain and Bealtaine are the strongest times of fairy influence and so are times when great care should be taken to avoid running afoul of them (Ó hÓgáin, 2006). At Bealtaine it was believed that the Fair Folk might travel abroad, appearing as a stranger at the door asking for milk or a coal from the fire; to give either would mean giving the household's luck away for the year to come (Wilde, 1991). At Samhain the Daoine Sidhe are known to move from one hill to another, from their summer to winter homes, and it is quite dangerous to meet them on a fairy road that night (Evans, 97). The Fair Folk are also especially active at twilight and midnight, and the slua sidhe, a kind of airborne malicious fairy host, is most active at night.

There is a long standing and complex association between the Fair Folk and the human dead, and indeed it is difficult to separate out the two groups in many cases. The dead often appear among the ranks of the Daoine Sidhe, especially the newly dead, and many stories feature someone seeing a thought-to-be-dead friend or relative in a marketplace. This is often explained by saying that the person had not actually died but was in reality taken by the Fair Folk and a changeling left behind, which was buried in the person's name (a common ploy with new brides and other attractive young people). The connection runs deeper than this though as the sidhe that the Fair Folk live in are often – although not always – ancient burial mounds, such as Sid in Broga, creating another complex layer of crossover. In many stories a person is believed to have died but appears, often in a dream, to a loved one and explains that they have been taken by the Aos Sidhe and can be rescued in a certain way, usually by the living person going to a crossroads at midnight when the sidhe will pass by in a procession and grabbing their loved one from the horse he or she is riding (Ó hÓgáin, 2006).

Offerings to the Daoine Sidhe traditionally include milk, butter, and bread, left by the doorway or at the roots of a fairy tree, as well as a bit of whatever one is drinking poured out onto the ground (Estyn Evans, 1957). Additionally, milk might sometimes be thrown in the air for the fairies or butter buried near a bog as an offering to them (Ó hÓgáin, 1995). At holy days it was also a custom to offer a heavy porridge which might be poured into a hole in the earth or bread which could be left out or tossed over the shoulder (McNeill, 1959; Sjoedstedt, 2000). The custom of pouring a drink out is mentioned in *Irish Folk Ways*, and is something I was familiar with as a family custom; my grandfather would pour out a bit of his beer in this manner, and while my father didn't, that I know of, I've long been in the habit myself of offering a portion of anything I am drinking outdoors to the Good People. It was also once the custom to bleed live cattle on Bealtaine and offer the blood to the fairies (Estyn Evans, 1957). In a modern context people seem to offer milk, cream, bread or other baked goods, honey, and portions of meals, as well as alcohol. These things are never given inside a home, as it would be seen as ill advised to invite these beings in, and instead were always given or left outside, preferably near a location associated with them.

The Aos Sidhe can bless or harm people. Their gifts could be good and lead to great blessings, or they could be illusions which would turn to leaves or grass at dawn. The sidhe gaoithe (fairy wind) which was a sign of the presence of the fairy host, could bring illness or cause injury (MacKillop, 1998). Elfshot is another well-known fairy malady, a sudden pain, cramp, or stitch caused by an invisible fairy arrow shot into the body by angered member of the sidhe. Elfshot might also be used against cattle, who would slowly waste away after being struck (Ó hÓgáin, 1995). In many cases it was also believed that elfshot was a power given to witches, which they learned from the Good Folk – indeed many Irish and Scottish witches were thought to have learned both malediction and healing from the Daoine Maithe with whom they were believed to deal (Hall, 2005). Those who were considered friends of the Daoine Sidhe were often privy to special knowledge and taught things like healing and magic, or a musician might be given great skill (Ó hÓgáin, 2006). The Daoine Sidhe might appear as a stranger at the door seeking to borrow something or needing milk or a coal from the fire, alone in a field or wood, or might be encountered on the road; those brave enough to seek them out might choose to sleep on a sidhe, knowing that the result would either be blessing or madness. In the tale of Lus Mór, a man with a physical malady, sleeps on the side of a sidhe, hears the Good Folk singing within, and adds to their song in a pleasant way after which they reward him by healing him. When another man with a similar physical issue hears of this, he tries to do the same, only he offends the Aos Sidhe who punish him by doubling his affliction.

There are a variety of protective charms against the Fair Folk, far too numerous to get into here, but I'll offer some examples. To keep a new mother and infant safe a piece of iron would be kept near them, either under or above the bed. To get the Slua sidhe to release anyone they may have taken one should throw the dust from the road, an iron knife, or your left shoe and say *"This is yours; that is mine!"* (McNeill, 1959). Should a person be suffering from the ill-willing attention of one of the Aos Sidhe a fairy doctor or bean feasa must be found, that is a person with special knowledge of the Othercrowd, who can diagnose the exact issue, be it elfshot or fairy blast, and come up with the appropriate charm, chant, or herb to cure the person (Wilde, 1991). Tying a red ribbon on cattle or horses was thought to keep the Good Folk away, as was tying a rowan twig on to a cow's tail, or lightly striking the animals with rowan or hazel switches (Ó hÓgáin, 1995; Ó hÓgáin, 2006). Rowan and red thread are another well-known protection, as is anything made of iron, a material that the Fair Folk[17] cannot bear.

Conclusion

"Three candles that illumine every darkness: truth, nature, knowledge."

— *Triads of Ireland*

The Irish Pantheon, and indeed Irish pagan belief, is a complex and wide-ranging thing which encompasses a range of regional beliefs across many centuries. This creates a complex interaction of belief and practice that can be seen in mythology and folklore, and allows for a variety of modern interpretations. And yet we find a distinct thread running throughout it all which gives it some cohesion into the modern day, even if there are so many different viewpoints and understandings of the material. Those seeking to follow an Irish pagan path, of any kind, have a great deal of material to work with and a large corpus of myths and folklore to draw from, which have only been skimmed here; I strongly encourage those interested in learning more to continue this journey by seeking out the stories for themselves and making an effort to connect to the culture. It is impossible, in my opinion, to separate Irish paganism from Irish culture or Ireland; the myths and stories are anchored in the landscape and the language in ways that cannot be underestimated.

There is a beauty in the old myths and the folklore, and besides helping us understand the gods and Aos Sidhe these stories also speak to struggles that are very human and very relatable. We read about the beings we honour dealing with things that humans also deal with, from Brighid's grief for her son, to Óengus's love of Caer, to Lugh's anger over his father's murder. These are relatable beings and not only can we understand the struggles and motivations of these beings but we can believe that they too can understand the joys and pains of our lives. There is a reference in the Dindshenchas to a man praying to the Morrigan for success in a cattle raid so that he can win the hand of the woman he loves, and it's clear he did this because he believed she would help him, would understand his plight. These are beings that have experience with loss, success, and the range of human struggles, in ways that create connection with them. They shouldn't be mistaken as simply human – they are still gods and beyond our full ability to comprehend – but there is a comfort in knowing that they too celebrate holidays and have funerals and must fight for their freedom. We may not understand what it is to come from the Otherworld in ships that land on a mountain but we all at some point know what it's like to feel like an outsider in a new place. The gods may not know what it's like to live a truly mortal life, since they never seem to stay dead when they die in stories, but they do know what it is to experience the joys and tribulations that we experience in our lives.

In this book we have discussed the broad strokes of Irish pagan belief and have looked at the gods and Aos Sidhe and their stories, as well as the practices that enrich those beliefs and provide a foundation for spirituality and practice. Every person will relate to this material differently and will find a path forward from here in their own way, but ultimately, we are all seeking the same connection. We are all trying to find the best way to understand what information we have and to nurture our beliefs and practices in the most fulfilling way we can.

The land has stories for those who listen, just as books and storytellers and music can guide us forward if we let them. The Tuatha Dé Danann and the Aos Sidhe are still there, waiting – sometimes actively reaching out.

It's your choice where to go from here.

Appendix A – Terms

This appendix is meant to offer a selection of the common terms in Irish with their English translations, to help readers who may not have any Irish or who may find the use of Irish placenames and other miscellaneous words confusing. Hopefully this will offer a bit of clarity.

Aitainmneacha / Place Names
An Cheathru Chaol – Carrowkeel
Brú na Bóinn – Brugh na Boyne
Cnóbha – Knowth
Cnoc – hill
Connachta – Connacht
Cúigí na hÉireann – Provinces of Ireland
Dumha na nGiall – Mound of the Hostages
Laighin – Leinster
Lios – Ring fort, fairy mound
Mide – Meath
Mumhain – Munster
Ráth – Fort, ring fort
Sidhe – fairy mound
Sid in Broga – Newgrange
Sliabh na Caillighe – Loughcrew, literally 'mountain of the Cailleach'
Teamhair – Tara
Uaimh na gCat – Cave of Cats
Ulaidh – Ulster

Sofhroital na Sióga/ Euphemisms for Fairies
Aos Sidhe – People of the fairy hills
Bean Sidhe – fairy woman
Daoine Eile – Other People/ Other Crowd

Daoine Maithe – Good People
Daoine Sidhe – People of the fairy hills
Daoine Uaisle – Noble People
Fear sidhe – fairy man
na hUaisle – the Gentry
Tuathghinte – literally 'northwards people'

Go hilghneitheach/ Miscellaneous

Badb – name of a goddess also a term for a supernatural woman, witch, and crow
Bainne – milk
Banríon – Queen
Bean feasa – wise woman
Cailleach – name of a goddess, also means crone, hag, witch
Caite – elf-struck
Conriocht – werewolf
Déithe – Gods
Draíodóir – wizard, enchanter
Draoi – magic user, druid
Gaeilge – Irish language
Iarlais – changeling
Piseog – charm, spell, also superstition
Rí – King
Sidhe gaoithe – fairy wind
Slua sidhe – Fairy host
Taibhse – ghost, spectre, phantom
Tromluí – incubus, nightmare

Story Names

Accalamh Senórach – Colloquy of the Ancients
Aislinge Óenguso – The Dream of Óengus
Audacht Morainn – Testament of Morann
Banshenchus – Lore of Women

Cét-Cath Maige Tuired – First Battle of Moytirra
Cath Maige Tuired – Battle of Moytirra
Cóir Anmann – Fitness of Names
De Choppur in Dá Muccida – The Struggle of the Two Swineherds
De Gabail in t-Sida – The Taking of the Sidhe
Genemain Aedh Sláne – The Birth of Aedh Slaine
Lebor Gabala Erenn – Book of Invasions of Ireland
Sanas Cormaic – Cormac's Glossary
Serglige Con Chulainn – Wasting Sickness of Cu Chulainn
Suidigid Tellaich Temhra – Settling of the Manor of Tara
Táin Bó Cúailgne – Cattle Raid of Cooley
Táin Bó Flidais – Cattle Raid of Flidais
Táin Bó Regamna – Cattle Raid of Regamna
Tecosca Cormaic – Instructions of Cormac
Tochmarc Emire – Wooing of Emer
Tochmarc Etaine – Wooing of Etain
Tuatha Dé Danand na set soim – the treasures of the Tuatha Dé Danann

Appendix B – Further Reading

This book is by its nature meant to offer an accessible overview of a range of topics associated with Irish paganism. If you are interested in learning more about specific topics or deities, please consider the books listed in the Bibliography as well as the following:

The Waves of Manannán by Charles MacQuarrie
War Goddess: the Morrigan and her Germano-Celtic counterparts
    by Angelique Gulermovich-Epstein
The Great Queens by Rosalind Clark
Archaeology and Celtic Myth by John Waddell
Pagan Past and Christian Present in Early Irish Literature by
    Kim McCone
Works by Lora O'Brien, Courtney Weber, or Anthony Murphy
Online lectures by Dr. Jenny Butler or John Waddell
Websites including Mythical Ireland, CELT, or Mary Jones
    Celtic Encyclopaedia

In addition to these I myself have written a range of books on related topics as part of the Pagan Portals series from Moon Books:

Aos Sidhe
The Morrigan
Raven Goddess
Brigid
The Dagda
Lugh
Manannán
Irish Paganism
Gods and Goddesses of Ireland

Endnotes

1. I personally do not like the term Celtic, which is often misused in paganism, but in this instance I am using it because it is the term that the community itself uses. My own usage would lean more towards Celtic language-speaking with an understanding that each individual culture within that is unique, rather than the widespread use of the word as an umbrella term for one unified culture that never really existed as such.
2. There is no evidence of any sort to support this theory beyond romanticism.
3. The modern spelling of this word is sí and the old Irish is sid or side, however, the antiquated 'sidhe' is popularly used and recognized so will be used in this text as well.
4. People of the fairy hills, who will be discussed in depth in Part II, but who should be understood as looking fairly human, although possessing greater abilities.
5. The text uses the term 'Lachlann' which literally means Norse areas, but was sometimes used to simply indicate very foreign or even non-human or magical places.
6. Until it was struck by Cu Chulainn for failing to cry out for him or his foster son, after which it's said the stone remained silent.
7. Readers may be happy – or at least amused – to learn that in the Lebor Gabala Erenn, written down by Christian scribes, Ireland was the only place on earth exempt from the Biblical Flood, at least in part. This must have reflected the Irish scribes' feelings about their home, even within a Christian context.
8. A hypothetical deity whose name means sacred tree or sacred post.

9. I would note that the Dagda is Brighid's father in Irish mythology but Berresford Ellis chose to make them lovers in his story.

10. Discussed in depth in Chapter 6.

11. Banb samna – literally 'young pig of Samhain'. Pigs were especially associated with Samhain and are repeatedly listed as the main animal to be used for the feast at this time (Kelly, 1997; Patterson, 1994).

12. It was a particular folk practice of saint Martin's Day, 11 November, to bleed the cattle on or near a fairy fort. The idea seeming to be that voluntarily giving some of the cows' blood would keep the Good Folk from taking the cattle entirely.

13. The folk beliefs vary across Ireland in ways that can be contradictory, so that the tree that should never be cut and brought inside in one area, lest it draw the Fair Folk, is the same one recommended elsewhere to protect against them. Similarly one area might believe that keeping dirty water in the home draws fairies and grants them entrance while another area believes this water drives them away. This can make it difficult to say almost anything with absolute certainty as there are nearly always exceptions.

14. Portions of this are also covered in my book *Living Fairy*.

15. Previously discussed in my first book, *Where the Hawthorn Grows*.

16. These sorts of pseudohistorical explanations for mythic beings is very common and is a form of euhemerization wherein spirits or gods are explained as a mere-humans and anchored within a classical world context.

17. At least, some of them can't and iron is the most widely recommended protection.

Bibliography

Banshenchus (nd) retrieved from http://www.maryjones.us/ctexts/banshenchus.html

Bitel, L., (1996) *Land of Women*

Briggs, Katharine, (1978) *The Vanishing People: Fairy Lore and Legends*

Butler, J., (2021) 'Brigit, Goddess and Saint, and Birth Traditions' in *Birth and the Irish: A Miscellany*

Carey, J., (1981) '*The Name Tuatha De Danann*'; Éigse

Carmichael, A., (1900) *Carmina Gadelica*

Chadwick, Nora, (1970) *The Celts*

Cross, T., and Slover. H., (1936) *Ancient Irish Tales*

Da Silva, B., (2009) Saint Patrick, the Irish Druids, and Ireland Conversion to Christianity https://web.archive.org/web/20160304072255/http://www.strangehorizons.com/2009/20090727/da_silva-a.shtml

Daimler, M., (2015) *How the Dagda Got His Staff*

— (2015) *The Treasure of the Tuatha De Danann*

Danaher, K., (1964) Irish Customs and Beliefs

— (1972) *The Year in Ireland*

eDIL, (2024) *Electronic Dictionary of the Irish Language*

Ellis, P., (1987) *A Dictionary of Irish Mythology*

Evans, E., (1957) *Irish Folk Ways*

Evans-Wentz, W. Y., (1911) *The Fairy-Faith in Celtic Countries*

Gray, E., (1983). Cath Maige Tuired

Green, M., (1992) *Dictionary of Celtic Myth and Legend*

Gwynn, E., (1906). *Metrical Dindshenchas, part II*

— (1913) *Metrical Dindshenchas*, part III

— (1924) *Metrical Dindshenchas*, part IV

Hall, A., (2005) *Getting Shot of Elves: Healing, Witchcraft, and Fairies in the Scottish Witchcraft Trials*. Folklore, 116

Heidja, K., (2007) *War-Goddess, Furies, and Scald-crows: the use of the word Badb in early Irish literature*

Jones, M., (2009) Anu. Retrieved from http://www.maryjones. us/jce/anu.html

— (2012) Nuada. Retrieved from https://www.maryjones.us/ jce/nuada.html

— (n.d.) The Battle of Crinna http://www.maryjones.us/ctexts/ cathcrinna.html

— (n.d.) The Birth of Aedh Slaine. Retrieved from http://www. maryjones.us/ctexts/aedhslaine.html

— (2004) Tech Duinn. Retrieved from http://www.maryjones. us/jce/techduinn.html

Joyce, P., (1908). A Smaller Social History of Ancient Ireland. Retrieved from http://www.alia.ie/tirnanog/sochis/sochis01. html#iv

Keating, G., (1857) *Foras Feasa ar Éirinn*

Kelly, F., (1997) *Early Irish Farming*

— (2005) *A Guide to Early Irish Law*

Koch, J., (2005) *Celtic Culture*

Kondratiev, A., (1998) The Apple Branch

Laurie, E., (1999) 'The Cauldron of Poesy', Obsidian Magazine. Retrieved from https://obsidianmagazine.com/Pages/ cauldronpoesy.html

Leabhar na h-Uidre (nd) Retrieved from http://www.maryjones. us/ctexts/flidais.html

Leahy, A., (1906) *Heroic Romances of Ireland*

Lysaght, P., (1997) *The Banshee: The Irish death messenger*

Macalister, R., (1941). *Lebor Gabala Erenn*, volume IV.

— (1944) *Lebor Gabala Erenn*, volume V

MacCoitir, N., (2006) *Irish Wild Plants*

MacDonald, L., (1993) People of the Mounds. Dalriada Magazine http://deoxy.org/h_mounds.htm

MacKillop, J., (1998) Dictionary of Celtic Mythology

MacNeill, M., (1962). *The Festival of Lughnasa*

McCone, K., (1990) *Pagan Past and Christian Present in Early Irish Literature*

— (2013) "The Celts: questions of nomenclature and identity"; *Ireland and its Contacts*

McCormick, F., (2010). *Ritual Feasting in Iron Age Ireland*

McNeill, F. M., (1959). *The Silver Bough*, volume 2: A calendar of Scottish national festivals, Candlemas to Harvest Home. Glasgow: Maclellan.

Meyer, K., (1890). *The Wooing of Emer*

— (1906) the Triads of Ireland. Retrieved from http://www.ucc.ie/celt/online/T103006.html

— (n.d.) The Instructions of King Cormac. Retrieved from https://www.maryjones.us/ctexts/cormac3.html

Monaghan, (2004). *Encyclopaedia of Celtic Myth and Folklore*

Murphy, A., (2020) 'Brú na Bóinn: Myth and Astronomy', [video] YouTube https://www.youtube.com/watch?v=VC7YQSmuL-0

— (2024) 'Ancient Alignment: Stone Age cairn in Meath Points to Ancestral Tomb 94 kilometers away in Sligo', retrieved from https://mythicalireland.com/blogs/news/ancient-alignment-stone-age-cairn-in-meath-points-to-ancestral-tomb-94-kilometres-away-in-sligo

— (2024) 'The Cyngus Enigma'. Retrieved from https://mythicalireland.com/blogs/astronomy/the-cygnus-enigma

Murphy, G., (1956) *Early Irish Lyrics: eighth to Twelfth Centuries*

O'Brien, L., (2005) *Irish Witchcraft From An Irish Witch*

O Donaill., (1977)., *Focloir Gaeilge-Bearla*

O'Dubhain, S., (1997) The Elements of the Dúile. Retrieved from https://web.archive.org/web/20060819124649/http://www.imbas.org/articles/elements_duile.html

O'Grady, S., (1892) *Silva Gadelica*

Ó hÓgáin, D., (1995) *Irish Superstitions*

— (1999) *The Sacred Isle*

— (2006). *The Lore of Ireland*

Ó Súilleabháin, S., (1967) *Nósanna agus Piseoga na nGeal*

O Tuathail, S., (1993). *The Excellence of Ancient Word: Druid Rhetoric from Ancient Irish Tales*

P. Sufenas Virius Lupus, (2011) *The Hidden Imbolc* http://www.patheos.com/blogs/pantheon/2011/02/the-hidden-imbolc/

Patterson, N., (1994). *Cattle Lords and Clansmen; The social structure of early Ireland*

Ross, A., (1998). *Pagan Celts*

Sanas Cormac (n.d.) Retrieved from http://www.asnc.cam.ac.uk/irishglossaries/texts.php?versionID=9&ref=150#150

Sims-Williams, P., (2020). "An Alternative to 'Celtic from the East' and 'Celtic from the West', Cambridge Archaeological Journal. Retrieved from https://www.cambridge.org/core/journals/cambridge-archaeological-journal/article/an-alternative-to-celtic-from-the-east-and-celtic-from-the-west/4F186F087DD3BE66D535102484F8E8C3

Sjoestedt, M., (2000) *Celtic Gods and Heroes*. Dover Publications

Smyth, D., (1988). *A Guide to Irish Mythology*

Stokes, W., and Windisch, E., (1897) *Irische Texte*

Stokes, W., (1894) *The Prose Tales of the Rennes Dindshenchas*

The Sidhe., The Tuatha de Danaan, and the Fairies in Yeats's Early Works http://www.csun.edu/~hceng029/yeats/funaro.html

Waddell, J., (2014). *Archaeology and Celtic Myth*

Wilde, E., (1991) *Irish Cures, Mystic Charms & Superstitions*

Williams, M., (2016) Ireland's Immortals

The Wooing of Emer (n.d) http://www.ucc.ie/celt/online/T301021/text056.html

Yeats, W., (1966) Celtic Twilight

Other Books in the *Pantheon* Series

The Egyptians
Robin Herne
978-1-78535-504-2 (Paperback)
978-1-78535-505-9 (e-book)

The Greeks
Irisanya Moon
978-1-78535-506-6 (Paperback)
978-1-78535-507-3 (e-book)

The Minoans
Laura Perry
978-1-80341-627-4 (Paperback)
978-1-80341-914-5 (e-book)

The Norse
Morgan Daimler
978-1-78904-141-5 (Paperback)
978-1-78904-142-2 (e-book)

The Romans
Rachel Roberts
978-1-80341-682-3 (Paperback)
978-1-80341-930-5 (e-book)

The Welsh
Mhara Starling
978-1-80341-742-4 (Paperback)
978-1-80341-741-7 (e-book)

Bestsellers from Moon Books

Keeping Her Keys
An Introduction to Hekate's Modern Witchcraft
Cyndi Brannen
*Blending Hekate, witchcraft and personal development
together to create a powerful new magickal perspective.*
Paperback: 978-1-78904-075-3 ebook 978-1-78904-076-0

Journey to the Dark Goddess
How to Return to Your Soul
Jane Meredith
*Discover the powerful secrets of the Dark Goddess and
transform your depression, grief and pain into healing
and integration.*
Paperback: 978-1-84694-677-6 ebook: 978-1-78099-223-5

Shamanic Reiki
Expanded Ways of Working with Universal Life Force Energy
Llyn Roberts, Robert Levy
*Shamanism and Reiki are each powerful ways of healing; together,
their power multiplies. Shamanic Reiki introduces techniques to
help healers and Reiki practitioners tap ancient healing wisdom.*
Paperback: 978-1-84694-037-8 ebook: 978-1-84694-650-9

Southern Cunning
Folkloric Witchcraft in the American South
Aaron Oberon
*Modern witchcraft with a Southern flair, this book is a
journey through the folklore of the American South and
a look at the power these stories hold for modern witches.*
Paperback: 978-1-78904-196-5 ebook: 978-1-78904-197-2

Readers of ebooks can buy or view any of these bestsellers by clicking on the live link in the title. Most titles are published in paperback and as an ebook. Paperbacks are available in traditional bookshops. Both print and ebook formats are available online.

Find more titles and sign up to our readers' newsletter
www.collectiveinkbooks.com/paganism

For video content, author interviews and more, please subscribe to our YouTube channel.

MoonBooksPublishing

Follow us on social media for book news, promotions and more:

Facebook: Moon Books

Instagram: @MoonBooksCI

X: @MoonBooksCI

TikTok: @MoonBooksCI